2003

W9-AFG-359

HOW WE WILL LEARN IN THE 21ST CENTURY

JUDY BRECK

A SCARECROWEDUCATION BOOK

The Scarecrow Press, Inc.
Lanham, Maryland, and London
2002

A SCARECROWEDUCATION BOOK

Published in the United States of America
by Scarecrow Press, Inc.
A Member of the Rowman & Littlefield Publishing Group
4720 Boston Way, Lanham, Maryland 20706
www.scaroweducation.com

PO Box 317
Oxford
OX2 9RU, UK

British Library Cataloguing in Publication Information Available

Library of Congress Cataloging-in-Publication Data

Breck, Judy, 1936–
 How we will learn in the 21st century / Judy Breck.
  p. cm.
"A ScarecrowEducation book."
Includes bibliographical references and index.
ISBN 0-8108-4310-2 (cloth : alk. paper) — ISBN 0-8108-4303-X (paper : alk. paper)
 1. Educational technology. 2. Information technology. 3. Learning. I. Title.

LB1028.3 .B72 2002
371.33′4—dc21   2002024018

⊗™ The paper used in this publication meets the minimum requirements of American National Standard for Information Sciences—Permanence of Paper for Printed Library Materials, ANSI/NISO Z39.48-1992.
Manufactured in the United States of America.

For Other People's Children

CONTENTS

PREFACE

This book is about a new era we are beginning to experience. Although there are things we can do to further speed its advance, several of which are discussed here, the new way we will learn in the 21st century is developing quickly on its own. Education woes are dissipating into enlightenment and it will not be long before terrorism will find an evaporated pool of youth to hypnotize. Elitism of knowledge will end as the mind of each citizen of Earth can freely learn from a common stock of everything known by humankind.

If you are about to dismiss me as a bemused optimist, I assure you that is not the case. For one thing, what I describe about changes for learning is observation, not speculation. Since 1996 I have been engaged in the digitization of academic knowledge and its interfacing onto the Internet. These efforts included leading the conception and construction of the contextual collection of 35,000 study subjects called HomeworkCentral.com, now part of bigchalk.com. My Web site EdClicks.com continues as a showcase of study disciplines available on the Internet and points to many illustrations of the online learning phenomena described in this book. Beginning in 2001, I have been participating in the development of a wireless content network that employs the nonlinear potential of the Internet described in these pages.

But there is another basis for my optimism that I hope you will take to heart in your own forward thinking, particularly in the dreary discussion these days about education. Things can get better; the status quo can change completely—a truth that is often difficult for younger people to realize. Being born in 1936, I entered the world at a perfect time to watch big bad things go away. I remember my mother saying how wonderful it was to be able to look at school playgrounds and see that all the children were beautiful. She was born in 1910, and would tell me that when she was little there were always kids around with crooked teeth and backs, those who limped and had club feet, and others who were frail or pockmarked. By the time I was old enough to have the conversation with her it was obvious from looking at playgrounds that there were cures in place for just about all the causes of the childhood infirmities Mother remembered. My first childish memories of economics are of my father's dream that he would take the family on a trip around the world replaced by war and rationing and learning to read the price of foods on a café menu so as not to order something expensive. I survived a childhood in the first half of the 1940s when toys were not manufactured at all and we never saw a piece of bubblegum. None of the other difficulties in ensuing years has stemmed the wealth in toys and treats children have since enjoyed!

By the time my understanding of the world became grown-up, the Iron Curtain had slammed down and threat of attack and foreign domination was terrifying. I remember shuddering by the radio listening to a dramatization of the dreadful novel *1984*. On the day the United States began bombing in earnest at the commencement of the Korean War, my family was visiting Los Alamos where my father knew some of the scientists. My parents went to a party that night at the home of Dr. Edward Teller, who they later told us kept going outside to see if Russian planes were coming up through Mexico to bomb the laboratories down the street. It was top secret then, but Teller was working on the hydrogen bomb. The night we were in town, he thought Russia might well be sending its air force to bomb the United States because, he said, "this would be their last chance . . . if they don't do it now they won't have another opportunity." Teller did not tell his dinner guests what he was doing in the labs, but he assured them that Los Alamos would be a prime target. My parents panicked, put us children in the car and drove back to El Paso. They soon turned our swimming pool into a bomb shelter. It was not long before intercontinental ballistic missiles were made operational, causing the ongoing possibility of obliteration from afar. It seemed certain that I was destined to spend my lifetime in a bipolarized world increasingly threatened by Big Brother.

By the real 1984, times were different. Like the once ugly children on the playgrounds of my mother's memory, most of the tyrannical players on the world scene were looking better. As the images of the Berlin Wall being torn down filled television screens in November 1989, I watched and wept with relief. The debilitating threat of world tyranny that had dampened my expectations for decades was over!

Have you noticed that senior citizens these days are flexible, often out-of-the-box thinkers? That is because my generation has learned, with good reason, to expect change. We now live in times that would not recognize the world we first entered. We ask you: Why not expect that within a few years the status of literacy and education we now know and lament will be unrecognizably different from their present sorry states? There are certainly no playgrounds out there that beg so tragically for cures as the ones filled with kids crippled by ignorance! We do profound disservice to coming generations to expect or accept a world where billions of minds continue to be wasted by their emptiness. My goal in this book is to show you that the future will be much different and better and to exult that the change is underway, inevitable, and wonderful.

Telling this story has been a great pleasure for me and I hope it will engage you in applauding and implementing the new ways we will learn in the 21st century. I am grateful to Tom Koerner, editorial director at ScarecrowEducation, for his encouragement and guidance that have made the book possible.

The book is dedicated with joy to other people's children at a time when the digital age is dissolving their divisions in intellectual opportunities from those of kids we may call our own. Putting a premium on one's own kids is natural and appropriate. Still, choosing among children is a distasteful matter. The truly radical surprise in the new way we will learn is that it allows all children, and all learners of any age, to imbibe knowledge equally from a common location used in common. That is at least as enormous as other changes I have personally watched, such as men walking on the moon, the Berlin Wall coming down, genomics (I was out of college before DNA made it into the textbooks) and the advent of the Internet. If you are already contributing to the new ways of learning, as many people are in many fields of technology and cognitive content, what you are doing is helping your own children and all present and future persons who learn. The Internet is the happy surprise making that true, as we will explore.

I do want to single out some children I have known and here thank them for their inspiration and their confirmation to me of the faith in all kids that I express in these pages. First, I remember the debaters I coached in 1960–61 at El Paso High School, grandparents by now, who showed me the raw power of adolescent thinking. The young teenagers whom I later taught for a decade in the communicant classes at the Fifth Avenue Presbyterian Church revealed to me the elevated honesty and reflective elegance of young minds. More recently, the debaters at Martin Luther King Jr. High School, among whom I believe were the most intelligent youngsters of my teaching experience, dazzled me with their intellectual ingenuity, tenacity, and valor. I learned from all of these encounters that kids rise to the highest mental goals you set before them. The implications from that are astonishing as the Internet is now removing all the barriers from learning.

ACKNOWLEDGMENTS

Most of the drawings and photographs are taken from collections kept by the author's grandparents and great-grandparents. The rest were created by the author and include two digital images based on Rembrandt etchings.

Supplementing this book, EdClicks.com provides a way for the author to keep the topics fresh and up-to-date and to give the reader online examples to explore interactively how learning is accomplished on the Internet.

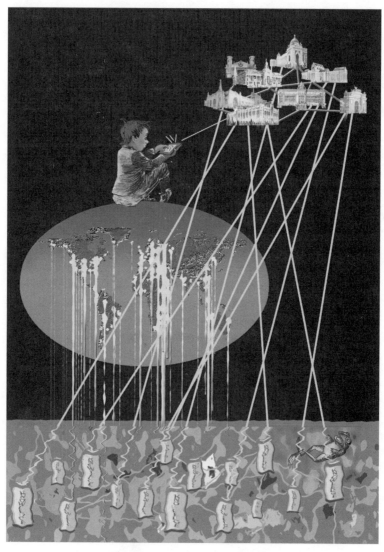

Figure 1.1. 21st-century learning

1

THE INCREDIBLE ECONOMY OF DIGITAL KNOWLEDGE

Singularity of Scale

Figure 1.1 is the whole book. The student sitting on top of the world has entered the new golden age of learning as he taps into human knowledge from the global common resource of the future. The chapters ahead explore the worldwide adventure of completing the transition to the way things are in the picture. The useful knowledge of humankind will continue to pour into the golden swamp that is today's Internet. Cognitive interfaces to that knowledge will be designed with increasing innovation, driven by enhanced technical efficacy, and will come online to reflect human knowledge for everyone to absorb. A great exposition of these resources will emerge from the swamp mist and congeal within the cloud of the distributed Internet. Every kid on the planet will have a wireless device to beam into it all. The book tells you that this is happening, how it is happening, and, I hope, will enlist your thinking and help.

Underlying everything in the picture is singularity of scale: education in the 21st century is being reformatted by the fact that a single nugget of knowledge in digital form can scale to be accessed by everyone on the planet. The revolution rests on the simple pivot from mechanisms that distribute knowledge to learners to a turnabout where all learners can reach to a single source of a particular kernel of knowledge. Increasingly and inexorably, each kernel resides in context that is a spontaneous Internet phenomenon. Singularity of scale and the context it causes are stunning, transforming, and healthy. It is fascinating and fun to watch it take place as it has, for example, with a famous rock: The Rosetta Stone that served as the key to deciphering ancient Egyptian writing. With one brief absence for protection during the bombing of London, the stone has been displayed since 1802 at the British Museum. Until the museum placed its Rosetta Stone pages online, there were three main ways to learn about the stone and its role in translation of hieroglyphics: (1) go to London and visit the museum, (2) seek out a teacher or expert, or (3) read about it in some form of printed material. Now any person at any time can virtually visit the museum online, and from there link out into a web of context for history, decipherment, and other related knowledge. The need to distribute printed literature is disappearing for any of the knowledge presented on the museum's Web pages about the Rosetta Stone.

As limitations of language are lessened (many knowledge resources are already available in multiple languages) and access to the Internet becomes universal, the singularity of scale pivots how we will learn. The formation of an expert and whole presentation for every conceivable nugget of knowledge unfolds. To get the idea of the comparative richness and authenticity, recall the paucity of an introduction to the Rosetta Stone in a paragraph and a simple drawing in an elementary or high school textbook, and then look at the British Museum's online exhibit.[1] The shift from limited physical, geographic distribution of printed materials to everyone virtually visiting a single source does a good job of illuminating sloppy scholarship and relativism. Peer review and public review are without limit.

This singularity of scale, where any single resource can be studied by an unlimited number of people, is a new phenomenon made possible by the Internet. A very beneficial effect is that the cost of knowledge is the same whether one person studies it or billions of people do. It is actually an education initiative that is almost free. The host of a particular knowledge nugget need only figure out how to pay for it once—and Web pages cost very little. The singularity of scale also is made possible by the permanence of most knowledge. Think, for example, of the static nature of arithmetic or chemistry contrasted to fluid numbers of billions of children who need to learn it now, all to be followed by younger sisters and brothers who are going to need to learn it next year and the year after that. There is just one pi that calculates the ratio of a circle to its circumference; billions of kids need to learn that it is 3.14159265—or they can all use the same online calculator to do their figuring. It is no exaggeration to point to a single digital multiplication tutor or interactive periodic table of elements that could be used by each and all of these billions of learners. Their use would incur no need to alter the original design unless a new element is discovered (a rare occurrence indeed!), and the cost for such a change would be one-time and minimal. What takes place can be compared to an image being captured by a camera: The image remains just one image whether viewed by a few people or broadcast to billions of viewers; you do not have to keep capturing more copies of an image in proportion to the number of people who see it. Contrast that economy to the effort and cost of publishing math and chemistry textbooks and distributing copies to millions of students, who wear them out in a few months or years so that the books must be replaced.

Knowledge that changes a lot is elegantly economical as well on the Internet, because of the singularity of scale to its users. It is far more practical and affordable to keep a subject like genome research, which changes daily and expands rapidly, up-to-date on one Internet gateway Web site than to print new materials and distribute them to researchers and students around the world—for whom the printed materials would be routinely out-of-date before reaching them.

Before discussing in detail the process depicted in the image in figure 1.1, its veracity needs to be explored. Can it be too good to be true? Or perhaps it is not so good if it is true. The next two chapters address some reasons that you may doubt the vision will become real or be beneficial. I raise issues about the ability of children to learn and the wisdom of machines becoming part of the learning process. But before going there we need to define that stuff pouring out of predigital knowledge repositories around the world, cascading into a mighty swamp, rising to palaces in a cloud, and beaming into the hands of the child: What is knowledge? That is very often the first question I get when I express my joy that students will soon hold it in their hands, delivered over the Internet.

I confess that it is an article of faith with me that knowledge itself is compelling— that we are lifted from baser concerns and freed by our intellect, a liberation I believe could be achieved by every person but that does not get the main attention in the actuality of education today. Anatomists say a human brain can be thought of as three brains, constructed something like a golf ball with layers wrapped around a center,[2] as suggested whimsically in figure 1.2. The brain in the center functions like that of reptiles and birds: it controls basics such as hunger, temperature, fight-or-flight fear responses, defending territory, and keeping safe. Wrapped around that layer is the part of our brain we share with mammals, including dogs, cats, and donkeys: major roles for this layer are mood, memory, and hormone control. Immersed as I have been during recent years in trying to explain my passion for the Internet's capacity at last to pour intellectual riches into schools, I had an odd thought when I read about the inner two brains. It occurred to me that what kids experience in schools too often is limited mainly to attempts to develop (or dominate) their inner two brains. These attempts are talked about in the same lingo as the brain functions! Much of the focus in classrooms is on hunger, temperature, fight-or-flight fear, defending territory, keeping safe, mood, memory, and hormone

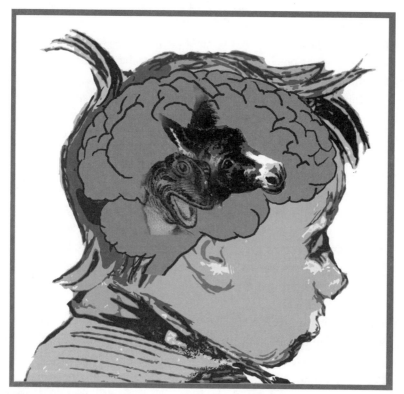

Figure 1.2.   A whimsical depiction of the layers of the human brain: reptilian, mammalian, and human higher cortex.

control. Some of the issues affect mainly disadvantaged schools, but many of them are major concerns even in the most elite academies.

A chief activity that occupies the third and outer brain, the cortex, is acquiring knowledge and thinking about it. But then, what is knowledge? The answer seems very simple to me, and I hope it does for you. It should be particularly easy to understand when we are talking about the knowledge that is crucial for a young person to acquire to participate fully in society. It is knowing how to read and write, use arithmetic, find something on a map, listen in an informed manner to a politician, and perform a job that creates value. Beyond these basics, I view knowledge as the substance of an expanding life of the mind that is one of the enormous pleasures of being human. Intellectual expertise is exciting and fun, whether it is winning the spelling bee, excelling at chemistry, or knowing the sonnets of Shakespeare. My teaching experience tells me that while participating in quests for knowledge, the happy purring of their cortexes tends to quiet the reptilian and lower mammalian urges of students.

Knowledge is the substance flowing down from the world depicted in figure 1.1. What the Internet will do to and for education is about knowledge, not about technology. The change is not the wiring or wireless beaming. The change is what comes over the wires and soon on radiant frequencies into the hands and minds of children everywhere: it is what is known by humankind. Newer even than the technology is a virtual presence of something within it that will educate everyone.

The human knowledge that has cascaded onto the Internet is cognitive content. Technology is a vehicle, not its passenger. Scientists, authorities in the humanities, research and reference specialists, artists, and a wide range of content folk are the prime architects of the transformation of knowledge into digital form. Moreover, what they are doing is quite recent and thus new and little-observed. The new cognitive change represented by the comprehensive removal of ideas, facts, formulas, images, narrations, essays, artifacts, and other vehicles of thought from books, libraries, museums, and the minds of the knowledgeable into interactive digital interfacing was not possible before the Internet became massive enough and its web thick enough to begin to reflect the richness of human thought. Modems had to speed up too, allowing memory-rich Web pages to find their way quickly onto monitor screens. Human knowledge is a cognitive web spun by our species over thousands of years, and spun internally in part by each of us as we learn and think over our lifetime.

Human knowledge is being woven and intertwined within the Internet. I am certainly not the first to envision the digital medium as a cognitive conveyance. Very early on, Apple's Hypercard software provided a tool for using the new interactivity offered by the medium in interfacing knowledge for teaching. The visionary folks who made educational CDs in the 1980s and 1990s developed further the potential of digital interfacing of knowledge. The Internet, of course, had been a means of exchanging academic knowledge from its inception, but exchange is not the same as being the primary location of knowledge, and the early Internet was merely a way to send things back and forth. While industry after industry was transformed by computers, it did not happen that quickly for the essence of education: teaching and learning knowledge. Why? We say the educators have dragged their feet, that schools have lacked initiative or are corrupted, that the government has not helped or has tried to do too much, that we do not pay teachers enough and the private sector is not attentive enough, that the parents have been neglectful—we even sometimes blame the kids because they seem to use computers just to play violent games.

My answer is that technology did not transform learning because the change for education that computers would launch would be cognitive, not technical. The computers could crunch numbers, process text, display images, and burn printing plates with elegance and power—but education products paled. The reason is simple in retrospect: Interactive lessons and CD tutorials were severely limited in the amount and complexity of content and context they could present, and cognitive content is essentially complex and imbedded in context. You would learn only a little bit from the interactive lesson or CD after the initial gee-whiz moments of admiring how cool they were when you opened them for the first time. Pretty soon you would think, to really learn this—to know it—it would be more helpful to read the book or let the teacher demonstrate.

There was another fundamental limitation: The cognitive substance of a digital learning product within a discrete digital file or burned onto a CD is trapped within its particular sequences of zeroes and ones and is not linked to its cognitive context. You can move around within it in exciting, nonlinear ways, but you cannot travel outside the file or over the edge of the disk to extend your cognitive experience. That is equally true of a book—you must put down one and pick up the next. Interestingly, it is not true of what goes on inside of your head, where you can jump around effortlessly from a day in childhood to a time decades later, from Bombay to Berlin to Boston, and from a mathematical formula to a phenomenon at the edge of the universe that you suspect the formula might describe. Your cognitive powers are nimble and quick. They are measured by how much knowledge you have acquired. The more you know, the more places there are that you can connect in your head.

The root meaning of the word *cognition* is "to know." Cognitive science emerged as a study discipline in the 1970s to focus on human perception, thinking, and learning. Not until the Internet reached an enormous scale have we turned the corner to experience the power and elegance of digital media to interface cognitive material. Something comparable to what goes on inside of your head has begun to happen on the Internet. The more knowledge available on the Internet, the more connections can be and are being made. The key to the cognitive facilitation here is the interplay of singularity of scale with multiplicity of connections: a singular best nugget of knowledge is not backwashed with duplicates, but instead is raised to prominence by the many connections it makes because its meaning is valid and useful. This marvelous cognitive capacity of the Internet enters a world used to thinking about education and computers as a matter of technology. That mindset is so pervasive that school librarians have taken the new title of technology specialist. Ambitions for computers in education trigger determination to wire schools, and that is about where it ends. Knowledge nuggets on the Internet are perceived in education projects as add-ons to textbooks and curricula. Distance education has developed as a process of connecting through the Internet, not primarily reaching into it. Meanwhile the cognitive powers of the Internet itself are growing and being refined inexorably by fascinating aspects inherent in its maturation.

What has at last now made computers a transforming boon for education is the enormous dimension the Internet has achieved, which now provides enough interconnectivity and complexity to reflect human knowledge. Not as a brain itself, but as nothing more than the enormous communication network that it is already, the Internet has become the primary warehouse for the product of human cognition, which is the pure gold of knowledge. The cognitive benefits are to our brains and those of our children: they will know more and can learn anything they choose. Beyond e-mail and commerce, among the information—meaningful only to humans—already stored out there is just about everything we have ever known: science, math, history, literature, language, and all the rest. The Internet stands poised to reflect all that back to every student on the planet. It is already happening.

CHAPTER 1

NOTES

1. British Museum Web site, www.thebritishmuseum.ac.uk/compass/index.html [accessed 21 June 2001].
2. Psycheducation.org. www.psycheducation.org/emotion/triune%20brain.htm [accessed 26 August 2001].

2

THE GREAT RELEASE OF WHAT IS KNOWN

Deus ex Machina

Change usually is a surprise, so much so that making things change is made difficult by a general disbelief that change can and will happen. Looking into the future it is hard to imagine how things will ever be different, and it is easy to act on the assumption that change has not happened and will not happen. Looking into the past is instructive: massive and pivotal change is commonplace. The promises made on the century-old advertising card for Carter's Little Nerve Pills in figure 2.1 demonstrate the point.

When the card was printed, Sigmund Freud was middle-aged and in the throes of his life's work of establishing modern psychology and psychiatry. Although British physician James Parkinson had described symptoms of "shaking palsy" in 1817, the underlying cause of Parkinson's disease was a mystery until the 1960s when it was associated with the loss of brain cells that produce dopamine, which helps control muscular activity. Perhaps it is as true as ever that dyspepsia (digestive distress) makes you nervous, and nervousness makes you dyspeptic. What absolutely dates the little card are its drawing, and language that today would invite lucrative lawsuits. The card is in several ways a clear demonstration that times have changed. That times can, will, and have changed is the message of this book.

The Nerv card belonged to my great-grandfather Milo Roblee. He was a traveling man, as he liked to phrase it. He established a home for his wife and two

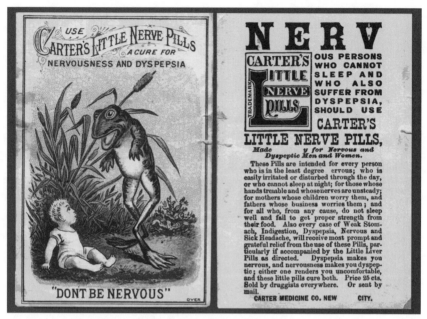

Figure 2.1. The copy on the lower right reads: These Pills are intended for every person who is in the least degree nervous; who is easily irritated or disturbed through the day, or who cannot sleep at night; for those whose hands tremble and whose nerves are unsteady; for mothers whose children worry them, and fathers whose business worries them; and for all who, from any cause, do not sleep well and fail to get proper strength from their food. Also every case of Weak Stomach, Indigestion, Dyspepsia, Nervous and Sick Headache, will receive most prompt and grateful relief from the use of these Pills, particularly if accompanied by the Little Liver Pills as directed. Dyspepsia makes you nervous, and nervousness makes you dyspeptic; either one renders you uncomfortable and these little pills cure both. Price 25 cents. Sold by druggists everywhere. Or sent by mail.

children in Topeka, Kansas, and from there spent the last quarter of the 19th century traveling throughout the United States selling sewing machines and other merchandise. I have a large box of advertising and social cards that he sent home from the road. Images from the cards appear in several figures illustrating this book. Milo Roblee's daughter married Dr. L. M. Breck, who grew up in Lawrence, Kansas, attended Washburn College in Topeka, and graduated from Kansas City Dental College about 1896. The postcards of the 1904 World's Fair seen on these pages were sent to the Brecks from the fair to their home in El Paso, where they settled in 1898. The images from my great-grandparents' cards are an ineffable demonstration of how very much times have changed since they collected the cards. Drawing styles have changed some, but the big visual change from their appearance to the images that surround us today is digital: the power of digital techniques to create and alter images is enormous. By way of illustration, the head in figure 1.2 is that of the frog from the Nerv card. I scanned the head from the original frog drawing, slipped it under a semi-opaque burro head from another card, and used them to suggest reptilian and mammalian sections of the child's brain. To create the fantastic image in figure 2.2, I used the same scanned frog head, processing it through some digital filters. That altered amphibian is an example of an idea in a changed package. It is a fine metaphor for the sort of change that is occurring for learning.

The positive changes in human learning described in the preceding chapter have come without planning, no one gets the credit, and they are a surprise. Realization is dawning about a related aspect: More people are getting access to more to learn. This sort of thing has happened before, when travel improved through wheels and boats, for example, and quite suddenly when the printing press was invented. The Internet is having the same effect as these early means of spreading knowledge, and that is wonderful. But there is something more—something that has never happened: everyone on the planet will be able to access and acquire common knowledge. A hint of what that would be occurred on 11 September 2001, when billions of people could view the same images of the towers of the

Figure 2.2. An extensively digitized frog

World Trade Center in New York City being struck, imploding, and falling. The images of that occurrence are imbedded in billions of visual cortexes and held in common by a large percentage of the Earth's population.

The media that delivered the images of the towers projected those images on television screens or in print. Everybody who saw them has an idea of what the real towers looked like. In the pages ahead a world will be described where everybody has access to learning just about anything and everything from a common source. As a few dozen cameras pointed at the towers at the time they were destroyed conveyed images shared by billions of people, there will soon be a few places on the Internet focusing each and every nugget of knowledge worth knowing, and every reasonable person who wishes to teach or learn these nuggets will use those few and excellent sources in common. That availability will expand exponentially as wireless devices morph from cell phones to Internet access and these handheld devices mature with heightened graphical interface sophistication. The knowledge these devices offer will become truly common when the price of the devices sinks, as has happened with television and radio, until every adult and child on Earth possesses one.

Proposing such a vision, as I have been doing since it caught me a few years ago, immediately raises the matter of convictions about children. A question that has long been a matter of (often heated) speculation will soon be answered: how many children are capable of learning very much? Never before could we know what would happen if everything that is known by humankind were readily available at virtually no cost to every child on the planet. Would Aristotles, Confuciuses, and Einsteins start sprouting up all over the place? We are about to find out. The *deus ex machina* who arrived on the stage of human history a decade ago has made finding that out inevitable. You may be among those who predict that there will be only a few more kids who really absorb a lot, because, you say, there is a bell curve that provides for only a few geniuses. But a few more geniuses alone is good news enough. Do you think there will be a few or a lot?

When I start making the predictions of more kids learning more by getting it from the Internet, these sorts of objections fly in my face: Children need nurture! They have to have teachers! They should not have pressure! They need to play and be socialized! Certainly, all of those statements are true. None of them have anything to do with the inevitability that everything known by humankind will soon be readily available to all children. Could a scrawny, dirty street girl of Bombay become a jurist? Is a five-year-old inner-city boy with a 200-word vocabulary a potential president of the United States? Those questions challenge common sense, stir deep-rooted prejudices, and raise sympathies that applaud minimal achievements. In the current clamor to express outrage at the failure of education, we are very long overdue in honestly evaluating educational equality for children. Rather than arguing the theories, I offer some anecdotes from my adventures and those of others with knowledge and kids.

Understandably, some of the smartest people I have known have found their own intelligence a hindrance to high expectations for all children. My most telling insight into this subject was demonstrated to me by the brightest boy then attending El Paso High School, in a classroom on a spring morning 40 years ago. It occurred as school wound down for the summer in the class where I taught debate.

Debate competition is a thread through my life that began for me in high school 50 years ago. These days I participate as a volunteer judge for tournaments in New York City and New Jersey. I do it whenever I can because I know it is helpful to the students who take part. Just as competing in high school sports can tone and strengthen young bodies, participating in forensic jousts can develop the thinking apparatus of young minds.

Debate was illuminated for me at a speech camp at the University of New Mexico during the summer of 1952, following my sophomore year in high school. We met in a wooden military-type building that provided temporary classroom space on the campus. As everywhere else in the early 1950s in the United States, there was construction. On the university campus, large postwar buildings were rising among the big trees and smaller prewar structures. The temporary classroom where I sat was bright and hot from the New Mexico July sun. I was enthralled by the man holding forth at the front of the room. I remember he used the word *truncheon* and I looked it up later. I recall that he was engaging, and sensed that he was giving me something very important. He was. This consummate debate teacher addressing the small group of New Mexico and West Texas high school kids who spent two weeks at the university in Albuquerque was Dr. James McBath. We knew he was a college teacher, and were impressed at the time by that. In later years I learned that he was a prominent collegiate debate professor and that his teams won major championships. He was located in Iowa, I believe, and later at the University of Southern California.

Dr. McBath taught me how to use the certainty of a conclusion in deductive logic to absolutely win a debate. It has frustrated me through the decades that the simple, deductive essence of debate can become clouded in wars of massive evidence. The principle Dr. McBath set out in that sunlit classroom is the reason his teams won championships. It hands the debater the elegant truncheon of deduction with which to clear the brush of muddled thought. It turns an awkward adolescent into an articulate advocate. But to have the wherewithal and courage to teach teenagers to debate that way, you have to both understand the tool and expect adolescents to think.

About the effectiveness of the tool, I have my proof. During my years as a high school debater I did fairly well, winning some local tournaments and the West Texas regional division with a partner. I did not continue debate in college. I believe I was a fairly typical teenage debater, and from the experience gained skills of thought and articulation that have been useful over the years. As a high school debate coach I was very successful, thanks to Dr. McBath. I was able to pass the truncheon on to two boys who wielded it with stunning skill. They won the Texas AAAA Boys State Debate Championship in the spring of 1961. Representing El Paso High School, they defeated the Houston team in the semifinals and the team from Dallas in the championship round. The boys, Fred Plog and Lee Projector, were high school juniors. No one won a debate against Fred and Lee after they began the rounds that concluded with the state championship. Texas was and is a major high school debate state and they won at the top level of high school competition. I did not teach school the second year they competed. That year they never lost a tournament and they again won state, because they had learned what Dr. McBath had taught me.

Fred was a brilliant young man. He was the first speaker when he and Lee competed in a debate. Fred presented the substantive case for the team and made notes of lists of questions as the opposition spoke. When he next spoke, Fred both reconstructed the position of his own team and sprayed the opposition with a withering volume of questions about their case. Fred was salutatorian of his high school graduating class, won a debate scholarship that put him through Northwestern University, and became a professor of anthropology. Lee was second speaker, rising after the substantive cases were essentially made to wield the full force of deductive logic. Lee's job was to pull apart the opposition's case and drive a truck through it. He was a joy to watch; he always came up with a devastating, fundamental flaw in the structure of the opposing side's reasoning. Lee also wrapped things up as second rebuttalist, making sure the flaw stood glaringly huge and obvious to the judges. Lee graduated from high school as valedictorian and received a scholarship to Stanford where he connected with hippiedom aborning and, I am sad to say, disappeared from my radar screen.

After their championship the first year, we had a couple of weeks left before school was out for the summer. Our early morning debate class spontaneously turned into informal debating sessions between Lee and me. He sat at the back of the room with his chair tilted against the wall. I stood in the front. The other kids, scattered in seats, chimed in now and then. Lee and I came to the same impasse over and over, and I learned something pivotal to my thinking from his intransigence (undoubtedly Lee saw our stalemates as my intransigence). But the sessions were good sport and our mutual respect was very high. Our exchanges toyed with the policy questions of the day: Should medicine be socialized? Should there be federal aid to education? JFK was president and the New Frontier excited young thinkers. Lee and I debated from our hearts. I gained an enormous appreciation of his compassion. I am confident there was never a time in his life when those around him, and he himself, did not realize that Lee was very intelligent. I could only be awed by this 15-year-old's stewardship of his exceptional mind. He wanted to put it to use helping others. The pivotal thing I learned from Lee was this: There was no way I could convince him that others could take care of themselves as well as he and other compassionate, gifted people could. My stubbornness in my debates with Lee was rooted not in my own conviction, although it is strong, that other people have an inalienable right to handle their own lives. The real difference of opinion was pragmatic. I think people's lives will turn out better when they control them instead of other people doing it. The smarter and more compassionate you are, the harder it is to believe what I just wrote.

It has always seemed to me that the key to how well people are able to lead their lives is what they are able to know. Certainly love and luck play huge roles. But it is the truth that sets them free and allows them to flourish. What Fred and Lee learned about debate was key in their lives—for Fred in providing his education, and I hope for Lee in permanent ways as well. Life would have been different for the boys if I had not gone to the speech camp where Dr. McBath gave me the truncheon of deductive logic. What if I had not taught school in 1960–61? Who gets the credit for the invincible Texas boy debaters of 1961–62? Dr. McBath? Me? Fred? Lee? To a major extent the truncheon of logic gets the credit. Deductive logic has an objective reality independent of any of us, and has been around for at least 2,400 years, since Aristotle was teaching it on a sunny porch in Athens.

A few years after I coached the El Paso High School debate team, a friend of mine who had debated in college mentioned Dr. McBath's debate fame and said he was known for coaching winning college teams. I always wished I could thank him for teaching debate to me. In 1997 I got back into debate, when I volunteered to coach the team representing Martin Luther King Jr. High School in the Lincoln–Douglas debates sponsored for New York City schools by Chase Bank. The following summer, George Soros' Open Society established a debate league for inner-city New York schools and King High School became one of the first schools to participate. Four decades after my summer session at the University of New Mexico, I found myself sitting at the huge conference table in King High School's law and justice studies conference room. I was surrounded by 16 subdued and nervous sophomores and juniors. They were going to spend the next three weeks at Emory University attending one of the top debate summer camps in the country. Other students there would be from Ivy League prep schools, big schools in Texas, and other places around the country with excellent debate programs and classes. I took some time to show the kids what a syllogism is:

All men are mortal.
Socrates is a man.
Therefore: Socrates is mortal.

I set two rectangular blocks on end and placed the third one across the top, explaining that the uprights represented the first two propositions, and if they did not stand up, the conclusion resting across them would fall.

As our session wrapped up, I told them not to be frightened or worried because no one at the camp would be smarter than they were. Do you believe that statement I made to them is true? I told it to them with no qualm or charity. I have known many of their peers and seen them in academic action, as for eight years I coordinated a partnership program between law firms and New York City public schools. The raw intelligence of inner city school students who turn out for programs that challenge their minds is no different from the physical talent of kids in these schools who show up for athletics. In both cases their gifts are often awesome. The major difference is that the opportunities for academic endeavor are far fewer and more talent in that area is wasted.

It was clear when school started in September that the experience at Emory had been as important for the King kids as mine at New Mexico had been for me. They won the first tournament conducted by the new league and participated with success and honor in the three successive competitions over the ensuing school year. Their coach was a teacher at their school, with volunteer help from me now and then. I also served as a judge at each of the tournaments. Several college professors from around the country attended the last tournament. They were observing as part of a proposed expansion of the high school program by the Open Society to other cities. One of the visitors was a dean of the Annenberg School for Communication—I remembered Dr. McBath had been connected with the University of Southern California, where the school is located. When I asked about the man who gave me the logic of debate the startled dean said he had been with Jim McBath when he died of a heart attack immediately after teaching a class. They had been close friends and the dean was still in touch with McBath's daughters. I told him of my admiration and appreciation for the enrichment of my life by the knowledge of debate logic Dr. McBath conveyed to me in that long-ago class. I asked him to describe Jim McBath to me, and the word that jumped to his lips was an "elegant" kind of man. And I thought, yes, I remember that.

Acquiring the understanding of debate that I have gave me a tool I have used often. Deciding not to acquire another useful body of knowledge played a major role in the direction of my life. If I had taken the place to which I was accepted in the University of Texas Law School class of 1961, I would have been doing something different in Austin, Texas, that spring. Instead of watching my team win the state debate championship, I would have been graduating from law school. Had I applied myself to practicing law over the decades that followed, I would have been a shoo-in for a federal judgeship by the 1980s. There are not many women born in the 1930s who sit today on senior judicial benches because, at least in large part, almost none of us went to law school. This is not meant as a reflection on Sandra Day O'Connor, who graduated from the same high school I did. I think she is much brighter that I am and I know she has more courage. When it came to attending law school, I chickened out. As I recall there were about 500 men in the UT class of 1961, and I would have been one of five women. I may be doing mental hyperbole in recalling the numbers, but I am fairly sure the proportion is about right and very certain that the reason I did not go to law school was I did not want to do a very odd thing in everyone's perception, including mine. Years later when the knowledge I would have learned in law school would be much sought after in a middle-aged woman, I could not become Judge Judy.

Ironically, in the early 1970s I witnessed up close the spectacular reversal of the dominance of women in schools of law. I was then working at a major Wall Street law firm as secretary to its managing partner. I simultaneously played the role that was the precursor of the now ubiquitous law firm legal recruiter. Unknown to the others (all men) who attended the meetings of hiring partners at the Association of the Bar of the City of New York, I was not a lawyer. (When they found out that I was not an attorney, they asked my boss to stop letting me sit in for him.) One of the meetings I attended was at the height of the on-campus fall interviewing season. In those days, attorneys from the Wall Street firms visited Harvard, Yale, Columbia, and a few other of the nation's most prestigious law school campuses. The competition among the firms for the top students was fierce. Although by the late 1980s, nearly half of the students that these firms hired were women, at the time of the meetings I attended, the challenge was to hold the number of job offers made to women down to just a few. There were still rules at the downtown clubs prohibiting women from lunching in the main dining rooms; adding a woman partner was not even a token consideration. The hiring partners had this problem: droves of extremely bright women were in the law schools and often beating out the men for rank and honors. The comment I remember at the hiring partner meeting that fall was shared as a joke and we all laughed. The partner said, "You won't believe it gentlemen, but last week on the campus I actually interviewed a dumb woman!" Are some of the smart women from those law school days now judges? You can be sure they are. One thing that makes them different from me is that I did not learn the law and they did.

Strident feminism has focused recent concerns about women more on their rights and less on their inherent abilities than in times past. The spring semester when I was teaching and Fred and Lee were winning their first state championship, my mother was running for mayor of El Paso. I would walk into my classroom to teach to find "What the heck, vote for Breck," scrawled on the blackboard. Mother ran against six men in a primary, got into a runoff with one of them, and lost by less than 2,000 votes. The point of the slogan, which some wag came up with, was that she was better than the men even though she was a woman. No one saw that as insulting; it was actually a compliment. It was also good humor and the Breck campaign had cards printed with it as a slogan.

By 1961, the consensus was that women were equally intelligent as men but should most appropriately apply their brain power to raising children or teaching school. If a woman "went to business," the position of secretary was an accepted role, and intelligence was expected from legal secretaries. The typical senior secretary at the Wall Street law firm where I began working in 1969 had received an excellent high school education from the New York Public Schools before World War II, but had not attended college. She was obviously very intelligent, and handled complex scheduling, tax filings, organization of legal files, and other duties that were to be taken over by young paralegals in the 1970s. Any knowledge these secretaries had about the law was obtained on the job, but it was acquired only around the edges and very rarely enticed any of them to seriously think of becoming a lawyer. Acquiring the knowledge necessary to pass the bar and practice law would mean getting a college education as well as going to law school—and law school for a woman was an odd thing to do anyway. These super secretaries, however, were highly respected and admired: What a great lawyer Alice would have made, if she had been a man! Do you agree with that, really agree? Or was Alice better off to have worked in the highest echelons of legal practice with the lions of Wall Street, as a secretary? Could she have gotten there as a lawyer? We cannot know the real difference there may have been in the potential of the boys (lawyers) and girls (secretaries) in the great New York law firms of the 1960s. But we do know this for sure: the boys had learned the law and the girls had not.

The consensus concerning the difference in level of intelligence between men and women was very significant as the 19th century began, and Mary Lyon did something about it. Her story is highlighted on the Web site of Mount Holyoke College, which she founded:

> With the birth of Mary Lyon on February 28, 1797, higher education for women gained an impassioned champion whose revolutionary vision would help transform the world. Lyon firmly believed that women must be well-educated to contribute significantly to society's greater good. This belief, fueled by her love of learning, inspired her to found Mount Holyoke Female Seminary.
>
> Lyon faced steep ideological obstacles as well. There were those who would confine women to the kitchen and nursery. It would be nearly a century before women gained suffrage (1920). Prevailing thought held, moreover, that women were constitutionally unfit to withstand the mental and physical demands of higher education. Lyon proved otherwise. She pursued the traditionally male discipline of chemistry and excelled. Her struggle to obtain an education fired her

determination to make higher learning available to all women, particularly those of limited means. . . .

With this remarkable achievement, Mary Lyon proved herself true to the words she would become renowned for: Go where no one else will go. Do what no one else will do.[1]

The college's history points out that Mary Lyon "instituted rigorous academic entrance requirements and a demanding curriculum conspicuously free of instruction of domestic pursuits." How well did the girls do? Were they as able to learn as boys were?

To take a direct and unbiased look, we next go to a previously unpublished example of Mount Holyoke class work. As you look through this essay, please judge it for vocabulary, grammar, sentence and paragraph structure, and essay skills. Then ask yourself how many college kids you know who can achieve at this level today. Here is an actual assignment completed by a girl in three hours in a class at Mount Holyoke on 15 April 1851:

A Trip to California

It was on the evening of the 26th of February that I left home in the company with one of my brothers for a trip to Eldorado. We were to proceed as far as N York and stopped there a few days to visit some friends and the principal lions of the place. As neither of us had visited that city before, we looked forward with much pleasure to our stay there.

We arrived at about eleven oclock and went immediately to the hotel, and the next morning after a good night's rest, we went to the house of our friends, & soon after sallied forth to explore the mysterious windings of that great metropolis. As almost everyone has been there and seen the wonder of the place, I will not stop to describe the many objects of interest which attracted our attention during the short time of our stay.

On Friday we went on board the steamer, and about noon we bade our friends farewell & soon with great rapidity we were skimming over the waters of the Atlantic. Everything went on pleasantly for several days. Many of the passengers were extremely sea sick, but we suffered very little from any kind of sickness during the whole voyage. It was necessary that we should put-out-to sea in order to avoid the storms, and danger of being driven upon the coast. But being driven by the wind farther to the eastward than was intended the voyage was made longer than we expected.

After having been out-of-sight of land for many days, only they who have felt it know how sweet the prospect of being once more permitted to step upon terra firma, and to smell the delicious breath of land.

Our captain thought best to stop at the island of St. Thomas, for the purpose of taking in supplies, and we all gladly embraced the opportunity of going ashore. The island is inhabited mostly by planters who employ the poorer classes of slaves. There are three mountain peaks, on which are the ruins of three castles— the one nearest the shore is said to be the one formerly inhabited by "Old Blue Beard" whose history has been the amusement & terror of children for so many years. He was said to have had two brothers, who lived upon the other two peaks, and having quarreled with them, he greatly distressed them by preventing their supplies of food and other things from reaching their castles. This he could easily do, as he was nearer the shore.

The climate of this island was very agreeable and every thing so new to us that we were very much delighted with our visit. We did not stop again until we reached Chagus. This place was occupied by the Spanish many years ago and the ruins of an old fort still remain. It is built of stone and must have been a formidable thing in its day. It is now overgrown with moss and shrubbery; some kind of fruit was growing upon small trees which hung over the water, and some of the men who were rowing about in the boat attempted to reach it but did not have much success. The town of Chagus is composed of a few low huts, and the natives present a squalid and miserable appearance. It was destroyed by fire a few years since and has never recovered its former size. We went inside of a building which seemed once to have been a church, but is now in ruins. Two large trees were standing in the center, and their tops were higher than the top of the building; the roof had long since fallen in. We passed up the Chagus or rather Nueces river in an open boat. The foliage of the enormous trees which grew upon the banks was richer than any thing I had ever seen before, while air plants clinging to their trunks and branches, and covered with flowers, rendered the scenery enchanting and filled the air with the most delicious fragrance. *Unfinished*

E. Starkweather[2]

The preceding essay was written by my great-grandmother Elizabeth Starkweather Breck, known to friends as Lizzy, when she was a 19-year-old student at Mount Holyoke. I typed the words into my computer, reading them off a blue sheet from the clear script penned by Lizzy's hand a century-and-a-half ago. I have no idea whether she actually took the trip or whether the story was fanciful. Clearly, she thought well of the essay because she kept it in her personal papers throughout her long life that ended at age 86. My father remembered visiting his grandmother Lizzy when she was an old lady and he was a little boy. He recalled with respect still edged with a youngster's awe that she could write in Latin.

As I typed the essay, I noticed a few light pencil corrections here and there. In the beginning sentence of the last paragraph the words "of this island" were added in pencil by a different hand. It looks as if the writing had been marked by a teacher. It would not have been Mary Lyon because she had died two years before, but Mary's influence was the guiding force of Lizzy's intellectual challenges at the college. If Mary, Mount Holyoke, and Lizzy could so beautifully demonstrate the capacity of women as well as men to learn and to flourish academically, why do all children not do so? Was Lizzy exceptionally gifted? Or are there other problems?

Mary Lyon's contemporary Horace Mann (1796–1859), known as "the father of American education," was well aware of some other problems. He fervently believed in the common school, meaning schools attended by all children in common, and now referred to as public schools. Mann was vexed that the reality of caring about other people's children had its limits. In 1846 he wrote:

There is not at the present time, with the exception of New England and a few small localities elsewhere, a State or a community in Christendom, which maintains a system of Free Schools for the education of its children. Even in the State of New York, with all its notable endowments, the Schools are not Free.

I believe that this amazing dereliction from duty, especially in our own country, originates more in the false notions which men entertain respecting the nature of their right to property, than in anything else. In the district school meeting, in the town meeting, in legislative halls, every where, the advocates for a more generous education could carry their respective audiences with them in behalf of increased privileges for all children, were it not instinctively foreseen that increased privileges must be followed by increased taxation. Against this obstacle argument falls dead. The rich man, who has no children, declares it to be an invasion of his rights of property to exact a contribution from him to educate the children of his neighbor. The man who has reared and educated a family of children denounces it as a double tax, when he is called upon to assist in educating the children of others also; or, if he has reared his own children without educating them, he thinks it peculiarly oppressive to be obliged to do for others, what he refrained from doing even for himself. Another, having children, but disdaining to educate them with the common mass, withdraws them from the Public School, puts them under what he calls "selecter influences," and then thinks it a grievance to be obliged to support a school which he contemns. Or if these different parties so far yield to the force of traditionary sentiment and usage, and to the public opinion around them, as to consent to do something for the cause, they soon reach the limit of expense where their admitted obligation, or their alleged charity, terminates.[3]

Fifteen decades have borne out the durability of these obstacles. Our instinct to provide for children is stronger for our own offspring than it is for other people's children. Who is to say that is a bad thing? If everybody took care of their own kids there would be no kids to worry about. Right?

Ten years younger than Mary Lyon and Horace Mann, Abraham Lincoln became a favorite example held up to children to prove the road to scholarship was open to all. The year before he was elected president of the United States, Lincoln described his school experience in frontier Indiana in these words:

> There were some schools, so called; but no qualification was ever required of a teacher beyond "readin, writin, and cypherin" to the Rule of Three. If a straggler supposed to understand latin happened to sojourn in the neighborhood, he was looked upon as a wizzard [*sic*]. There was absolutely nothing to excite ambition for education. Of course when I came of age I did not know much. Still, somehow, I could read, write, and cipher to the Rule of Three; but that was all. I have not been to school since. The little advance I now have upon this store of education, I have picked up from time to time under the pressure of necessity.[4]

Although he tended to apologize for a lack of learning, Lincoln managed to pick up a great deal of education essentially on his own, including training himself as a surveyor and a lawyer. He began reading as a boy, at first only a few books because only a few were available. He often read these books more than once, memorizing passages to make them a permanent resource for his thinking. The basic reason for Lincoln's very limited school experience was the remoteness of his family home. Books were just about the only technology that could overcome the distance to sources of academic knowledge. By the time he had reached adulthood another technology, the railroad, had reached the American Midwest. More books and more teachers arrived on the frontier scene to provide opportunity for young people to learn.

A Lincoln contemporary who did not become a positive example to posterity also wrested learning from extremely difficult circumstances. The *New York Times* obituary of the man who succeeded Lincoln to the presidency explains:

Andrew Johnson was born in Raleigh, N.C., Dec. 29, 1808. His father, Jacob Johnson, who was in the humblest circumstances, was drowned while attempting to save the life of Editor Henderson, of the Raleigh Gazette, in 1812, and six years later young Andrew, at the age of ten, was apprenticed to a tailor named Selby. School was then out of the question, of course, and the outlook was that the young man would grow up to an illiterate life. But the intellect that was in him was aroused through the instrumentality of a Raleigh gentleman, whose practice it was to read aloud to the tailor's employees from books of published speeches. The speeches of some of the British statesmen particularly attracted his attention, and he set about learning to read with the same determination which characterized his later life. By resolute application after work hours and in moments taken from sleep, he soon succeeded and was able to read the speeches and other books for himself. He left Raleigh in 1824, before his apprenticeship had expired, and went to Laurens Court House, S.C., where he worked two years at his trade, and then, after a return to Raleigh and a brief stay there, he removed with his mother to Greenville, Tenn. He soon married, and was fortunate enough to get a wife who was a helpmate to him in every sense of the word. She set herself at once to supply his greatest lack, became his teacher, giving him such oral instruction as was possible while he was at work, and teaching him writing, arithmetic, and other branches at night. Under her faithful tuition he acquired a fair education. The native forces of his mind supplied the remaining elements of his success.[5]

Lincoln, Johnson, and others like them learned what they could during a time when there was a given in the discussions of education that continued through the closing decades of the 19th century. There was a consensus that in a democracy, opportunity should be the same for all to climb the ladder of education to escape ignorance and poverty. Except for the Negroes, the ladder should be available to all children. You had to feel obligated only to the point of being taxed so that other people's children had schools to go to, yet if some of those kids managed to climb that ladder, you were glad for them and proud to be in a country where that could happen. The key idea that has since become murky is whether and how many kids were capable of climbing the ladder. The ladder collapsed when we muddled that belief enough that it became okay not to provide the opportunity because the children could not climb that high anyway. Compounding the difficulties described by Horace Mann are the declining expectations for children—which are at worst cynical and at best well-meaning excuses for allowing the dumbing down of education.

Take, for example, the wonderful gift of competitive debate that brings thinking triumphs for kids in every kind of school. Doubters worry that maybe only the brightest few can understand and handle debate; it may crush less-endowed youngsters to lose competitions to kids who are more able. Can all children become advocates? Can all children learn? We have been blaming governments, cultures, parents, and schools for the failure of children to learn. But maybe we also blame the children. Do you do that? Do you think all children can learn? Do most people think so? How many children are inherently not able to learn? We live in times of sagging expectations, represented by enthusiastic cheers when kids meet very low testing standards. Perhaps the most telling pointer to the decay of education optimism is the bandwagon for testing and standards. More and more of us are settling for less and less student achievement. Is it a sufficient victory to read at grade level?

In June 2001, Paul G. Vargas announced that he was leaving the job of chief executive of the Chicago school system. He was applauded for his accomplishments during his six years at the helm of the troubled system. As he was concluding his tenure, Chicago Board of Education member Avis LaVelle said, "We've picked the low-hanging fruit, and we've gotten on the step stools and gotten some of the fruit that wasn't hanging so low. But now we're going to really have to stretch."[6]

Here is the level of achievement to which Mr. LaVelle was referring: "About one in four Chicago students read at grade level when Mr. Vargas took over; now, it is more than one in three. Math scores have also improved, with about 40 percent of students at grade level, up from 30 percent. This year, high school reading and elementary math scores slipped."[7]

Half the fruit is rotting on the tree. Half of the children cannot read and half the children cannot do their math. Is it Paul Vargas' fault? Is Avis LaVelle calling children names? Messrs. Vargas and LaVelle are at least there trying and caring. We must be grateful to them for their courage to be in the fray, their concern, and their progress. Perhaps those children, who belong to somebody else out there in Chicago, are actually doing as well as can be expected. Do you think that? How many people actually believe the ones that are failing could succeed as students? If the same children who are in the Chicago schools had come through suburban schools where essentially every student achieves at grade level or above, would the kids from Chicago also have achieved at that rate?

Does being poor and living in wretched circumstances condemn a child to intellectual failure? That had not been true for Abraham Lincoln and Andrew Johnson. Does the following echo from Emma Lazarus still mean anything?

Give me your tired, your poor,
Your huddled masses yearning to breathe free.
The wretched refuse of your teeming shore.
Send these, the homeless, tempest-tost to me,
I lift my lamp beside the golden door!

The 20th-century history of public schooling in the United States is badly blemished when it comes to providing equal intellectual opportunity for all the nation's children. Futility began to set in for some of other people's children when the ladder everyone once could climb in common was laid down to become a road with forks that led bunches of students in different directions. It began to be asked whether all of other people's children were smart enough to go to college. If not, was it not more sensible to prepare them for vocations? Besides, would they not be frustrated and stunted by not making the grade while being outshone by brighter kids? Everything else can be placed on a bell curve, why not do it with children? We would save money. It would be more kind. Children from foreign countries, dangerous streets, and difficult homes bring baggage with them to school. We know it is not their fault. We should not expect too much and we should help them celebrate their small victories.

On the book's cover, *Time* magazine gives this praise to *Small Victories:*[8] "An upbeat book about triumphing against the odds. . . . The victories seem large indeed." The book is the compelling story of a teacher at Seward Park High School in New York City. Almost all of the students in this large, overcrowded school were immigrants and members of minorities. Located in lower Manhattan, the school's neighborhood was rife with drugs and crime during the 1980s described in the book, which paints a compassionate picture of other people's children in the terms of those times. Sixty years earlier, Cornelia James Cannon was more blunt about her opinion of the children of immigrants, who in her times would have looked a lot like those in figure 2.3. In a 1922 article in *The Atlantic Monthly,* referring in large part to children from Poland, Italy, and Russia, she lamented:

> They are persons who not only do not think, but are unable to think; who cannot help in the solution of our problems, but, instead, become a drag on the progress of civilization. In a society so complex as that which we are developing, they are a menace which may compass our destruction.[9]

Figure 2.3.   Advertising card for cotton thread, circa 1900

What do we really think is the potential for those children of other people in Seward Park High School and public schools of Chicago? Are their small victories really victories or truly just small? Two centuries of U.S. education have identified problems with educating what I have been calling other people's children with seeing to it that the ladder of learning stands tall for all children. I think history will record that providing equality in education became impossible in the 20th century.

The difficulties are not limited to the United States. A news story about the first delivery of humanitarian supplies into Afghanistan after the 11 September 2001 terrorist attacks illustrates the point. The dispatch explained that the supplies would be food, medicines, and some school books. They were to cross the border into Afghanistan in large trucks and proceed to an interior location where they would be transferred to a fleet of smaller trucks that would take them into the mountains. To cross the high mountain passes, the supplies would once again be offloaded from the smaller trucks and then strapped to the backs of 4,000 donkeys for the final phase of the trek. For millennia, knowledge beyond what is known locally has relied on physical transportation, and for the remote Afghan kids that meant donkeys and still does. Knowledge is burgeoning beyond their remote valleys, where it once sufficed to master tribal language, lore, and skills. Even now, if the mountain children of Afghanistan are to have knowledge of the 21st century sciences, humanities, and the rest, it will have to come in on burro backs, as it always has. My guess is that the last education-related delivery the donkeys will have to make is a supply of devices for the children of the mountains like the one the child is using in figure 1.1.

Through the upheavals, chaos, discoveries, and innovations of the 20th century, sciences, medicine, transportation, communication, agriculture, and other major human endeavors progressed significantly worldwide. Over the same period, the outlook for education slipped in fits and starts into a long slide toward insoluble difficulties. Collectively, humanity knows more than ever, but nearly a billion of our 6 billion global residents cannot read. Of those who can read, only a small number have acquired a lot of knowledge, because advanced schools are few, remain the privilege of the elite, and, in most regions, are composed primarily of men. The 5 billion-plus people who can read do, of course, have the essential qualification to pick up a handheld like the boy in figure 1.1. Singularity of scale becomes an intensely amazing idea when you realize that these billions may soon do just that, and they can then all share knowledge in common on single Web pages. Most of those 5 billion-plus people who can read are like Abraham Lincoln or Andrew Johnson who achieved those basic skills. We can be very sure at least some of them will use those skills and proceed to educate themselves, as did Abraham and Andrew.

In the United States the decline in learning has become more or less accepted. In a symbolic mirroring of what has become expected of our children's minds, an American century that opened with the design and building of architecturally magnificent school buildings closed with efforts to keep those same structures from falling down—in the midst of a record booming economy. It would be unfair and cynical to blame anyone for causing the stunting or ruin of the minds of millions of kids. As the slogan sighs: "A mind is a terrible thing to waste." My guess is that in spite of the best efforts of our best people, had the Internet not been developed, we would have continued to drag on through still more decades of discouragement. We will never know what would have happened because suddenly things are different.

As the 21st century begins, the central problem that children are not learning is solving itself. A new golden door is swinging open through which every child may pass to become intellectually strong and free. I believe I can show you in this book that the impact of new technology is fundamentally altering what education will be across the world, even in the most remote locations. Along with the change that will make education happen everywhere, we will experience a global migration from mediocrity to the highest level of learning ever achieved by our species, and that achievement will be by students throughout the world. We have begun the most compelling and exciting era of learning in all of human history.

Clearly a change that pivotal from our current frustrations requires a spectacular turn of events. The central event of education today is that a machine has arrived on the stage that has made everything different. Yet the new factor that swings open education doors is not technology or a machine. The transforming and wonderful turnabout for education is being caused by what a machine turned loose into cyberspace as the 20th century ended. It came as a grand surprise like a trick employed in plot debacles by playwrights in ancient theatre. It is the *deus ex machina*, which is, as Webster's[10] explains:

> 1 : a god introduced by means of a crane in ancient Greek and Roman drama to decide the final outcome 2 : a person or thing (as in fiction or drama) that appears or is introduced suddenly and unexpectedly and provides a contrived solution to an apparently insoluble difficulty.

The glowing, pulsing, crane of wires and light that delivers the god that caused the education change is the Internet. The *deus* is Pandora. The lady who lets all the stuff out of the box is back. Actually, in mythology she is not a god, but a human. The Greeks knew her as the first woman. She was fashioned in the image of an immortal goddess by the gods Hephaestus and Athena at the instruction of Zeus. All the other gods were commanded by Zeus to endow Pandora with special qualities, and she received many lovely gifts such as beauty, grace, and dexterity. Darker gifts were bestowed as well: from Hermes, the germ of falsehood and from Hephaestus, lying and deceit. I realize that the myths of Pandora are a put-down to women, but that is irrelevant here. The best story about her is how she opened the lid—and that is what she did to become the *deus* of the golden age of education.

There are two versions of how Pandora performed the act that has made her a favorite over the centuries of the tellers of legends and the makers of paintings. In one story, Zeus sent her to the Titan Epimetheus, a brother of Atlas. Another of their brothers, Prometheus, had earlier been tricked by Zeus through Epimetheus, and Prometheus had forbidden Epimetheus to accept gifts from Zeus. But Pandora's beauty overwhelmed him and Epimetheus made her his wife. The groom possessed an earthenware vessel containing all evils and only one good, hope. Pandora's curiosity about the pot soon led her to lift the lid. Everything quickly escaped, except hope, which was at the bottom of the pot. She managed to shut the lid before hope got away. In other versions of the story, Pandora brings the container with her as a wedding present, and it contains all of the good things that are blessings to humankind. Again, she lifts the lid and the contents escape, this time with all things that are good floating back to heaven, beyond human reach. In both versions, hope alone remains by the time Pandora gets the top shut, and by then it has become impossible to get the former contents back into the container.

Technology in the classroom is not the fundamental solution to our education woes. In the first place, the machine the students will use to learn is morphing into a wireless device not attached to the classroom but held in the learner's hand. In the dramatic plot change, digital technologies are the *machina;* it is the *deus* that the crane deposited on the stage of education that changes the plot. For the past decade, a very busy Pandora has been throwing open the lids on the containers of human information and everything known by humankind has flown off into cyberspace through the Internet, not to return to whence it came. I changed this a bit in figure 1.1: here the stuff flows into a swamp. The Pandora metaphor correctly reflects a spectacular, massive, and total outpouring of knowledge whichever way the story was told in mythology. Certainly the alarm is warranted by those who cry that bad things are loose on the Internet. It is equally true that all the good things are there. The Pandora tale is potent, for it reminds us of the reality of finality.

All the king's horses and all the king's men
Couldn't put Humpty together again.

Education must and is adapting to Pandora's new lid-lifting. The plot will veer away from the insoluble difficulties heaped up over the past century. We will never know if we could have reasonably improved the lot of all children within the world as it was before what could be learned by students cascaded onto the Internet. By mid-21st century, I believe we will be reflecting back to the birth of the Internet with questions about education like these: Could remote, impoverished, totalitarian countries and ghettos have experienced universal literacy had wireless devices not delivered polyglot reading materials? Would the global cultural fiber of mid-21st century have been so golden had anyone who wanted to not been able to see and hear all the art ever created? Could the Theory of Everything have been achieved had not every 10-year-old been exposed to mathematics? (Certainly the solution would not have come from a team cooperating between Mongolia and Uruguay.) Could the Socratic method have returned as the major technique for teaching teenagers without the free access to all knowledge on the Internet? Would teaching have become the most honored and coveted of professions without the emergence of digitally rich pedagogy?

Again the same question creeps into the picture: These things are wonderful for some, but can all children learn this way? That question is a powerful and operative factor in preserving a status quo that is increasingly frustrating and somber. Let us not blame the kids for a refusal to move into the future. We can do better than patching things up on step stools. The question we really need to answer is not can all children learn, but rather: how can we direct all children into engaging the study disciplines on the Internet? The reality is that the Internet is already the superior method for encountering the substance of learning. The proper activity for the designers and builders of future education is the engagement and enhancement of digital knowledge. It is interesting to speculate whether this means that all children will learn something, and we are about to find out. One thing that is certain is that the substance of human learning that flew out as Pandora opened lids will never again be confined. Things have changed.

The Internet is now and will remain for the foreseeable future the primary location of human knowledge. It has surpassed many times over the libraries, museums, universities, books, and human experts. A potpourri of highlights from these vast and beautiful resources appears on the Web site EdClicks.com. Most anyone would be confident that students like the debaters I coached in El Paso, Lizzy when she was at Mount Holyoke, and most of the debaters at King High School would jump into these resources and flourish as students. Some will believe that the low-hanging fruit in Chicago and the rest of the world's isolated and ignorant who find themselves limited as young Abraham Lincoln and Andrew

Johnson were, are unprepared to respond. I would disagree with that because I believe knowledge itself is compelling—but settling that is really not relevant here. It is going to be fascinating to watch. With a tip of the hat to Pandora, it is time to dispose of the pains of 20th century education by lifting the curtain on a reset stage and a brand-new plot. But before we can do that, we must deal with mechaphobia.

NOTES

1. www.mtholyoke.edu/cic/about/history.shtml [accessed 14 June 2001].

2. Papers of Elizabeth Starkweather Breck. Private collection.

3. Horace Mann, "Tenth Annual Report of the Massachusetts Board of Education," in *The Republic and the School: Horace Mann on the Education of Free Men,* ed. Lawrence A. Crimins (New York: Teachers College Press, 1957), 58.

4. From Lincoln's letter to Jesse Fell, enclosing an autobiography, 20 December 1859. Abraham Lincoln online, showcase.netins.net/web/creative/lincoln/speeches/educate. htm [accessed 15 June 2001].

5. Andrew Johnson obituary of 1 August 1875, *New York Times on the Web,* www. nytimes.com/learning/general/onthisday/bday/1229.html [accessed 20 July 2001].

6. Jodi Wilgoren, "Chief Executive of Chicago Schools Resigns," *New York Times on the Web,* 7 June 2001, www.nytimes.com/2001/06/07/national/07CHIC.html [accessed 7 June 2001].

7. Wilgoren, "Chief Executive of Chicago Schools Resigns."

8. Samuel G. Freedman, *Small Victories* (New York: Harper Perennial, 1990), cover.

9. Diane Ravitch, *Left Back: A Century of Failed School Reforms* (New York: Simon & Schuster, 2000), 141.

10. *Merriam-Webster's Collegiate Dictionary,* 10th ed. (Springfield, Mass.: Merriam-Webster 1997).

3

ADJUSTING TO
THE MACHINES
Mechaphobia

"It's a funny thing, but I have never had to show a little boy how to use a mouse." This comment was made to me in 1995 by a teacher at an upscale New York City private elementary school for boys on the East Side of Manhattan. The teacher was the technology specialist—and the entire technology department—for the school. Having had the job for three years in those early days when only a few select schools had been wired for the machines, he was a rare expert on how kids relate to computers. He said that every time he introduced the computers to a boy to whom they were new, he just put the mouse in the boy's hand and the child started moving and clicking.

In 1999, the head of technology for a New Jersey city school district showed a colleague and me the computer facilities in several schools. In the four years since my conversation with the New York teacher, technology had grown rapidly and been placed in thousands of schools around the country. Although the city I was visiting in New Jersey was not a wealthy one, computers were a strong presence in its schools. I mentioned to our host the teacher's comment about not having to teach little boys how to use a mouse. He laughed, and regaled us with his method for teaching 4-year-olds. He said, "You never try to tell her. That doesn't work." The effective technique, he explained, is just to put the mouse in her hand. First, he said, she will put it in her mouth, but that gets her nowhere. Then she will hold it up to her ear and listen, but that doesn't help either. Then she rubs it on her clothes. Soon, she will notice another kid nearby who has the mouse down on the pad, moving it around. So she will put it down and move it, and in no time will understand how that moves something on the monitor screen. Once she connects what is happening on the screen to her mouse, she will always know how to use the device.

The description of the little girl's learning process reminds me of how it felt when I finally knew how to ride my bicycle. We had a block-square park near our house. The park was grass-covered and had a downhill tilt across from a high corner to the low one. It was a perfect place to learn to ride my bike. Over and over, I would walk the bicycle up to the high corner, point it to the low corner, get on and try to gain control as the machine rolled downhill. Over and over I lost my balance, and sometimes I fell in the soft grass. Then in a quick moment, the control came. The machine and I were communicating through my kinetic sensory system. Decades later, those connections remain available.

Although riding a bicycle is far more dangerous to a child than operating a computer mouse, just about everybody thinks riding a bike is okay, but a phobia is awakened in seeing a small child staring into a screen and interacting with its contents. Steven Spielberg has given us a new word for the object of that fear: *mecha*. In the movie *A.I.*, Gigolo Joe, who is a mecha, as artificially intelligent robots are called in the film, explains to the little robot boy David that the term is from *machine* and that humans are *orga*, from organic. The etymology is sound: both *machine* and *mechanical* have their root in the Greek word for machine, which is *mechanikos*.

New York Times movie critic A. O. Scott describes how people think of mechas in the movie: "[David] and Joe are captured by bounty hunters and herded into cages at a Flesh Fair, a combination revival meeting and monster-truck rally at which people express their hatred of mechas by blowing them up and dousing them with acid."[1]

Clearly, the human beings who are destroying Spielberg's mechas are reacting to a different kind of machine than a bicycle. When the connections are kinetic and the machine performs physical work for us, the reaction is seldom fearful. I recall not fear, but gratitude, when I was able to ride my bike down the 10 gently sloping blocks between my house and my school. Coming home uphill was not as much fun and I usually was just lazy and walked the bike home. It was wonderful when I got my driver's license and another machine, a Jeep, whisked me effortlessly anywhere I pointed it.

Although it is very healthy for a teenager to fear being hurt while riding a bicycle or driving, I remember no fear from either experience—with one exception. The one exception to my fear-free years of teenage driving came from a very close call one school day morning when I was 16-years-old. About 7:30, I was blithely roaring up a quiet street in my Jeep through an intersection that had no stop sign for any direction. I had seen no other vehicle at all that morning when I suddenly realized I was well into the intersection and a car was about to broadside me from the right. I pushed the accelerator to the floor, pulled the steering wheel to the left, bounced over a curb and headed straight toward a 10-foot-high rock wall. I pulled the steering wheel madly to the left. The Jeep spun all the way around, missed the wall by about a foot, went back over the curb, and stopped in the street, leaving deep tire ruts in the lawn between the curb and the wall. I don't remember what the other car did after my wild spin and assume it just kept going after I swerved. I do remember realizing no one seemed to have seen me make such a fool of myself. My immediate reaction was to continue driving to school as if nothing had happened. For months, when I drove—always with extra care—through the intersection, I could see the U-turn shaped gouges the Jeep's wheels had made in the lawn when I jumped the curb. I was the only one who knew how they got there, and was not about to tell anyone about them. There was also a deep groove etched in my brain. It is a useful and justified fear of unprotected street intersections.

Spielberg's movie mechas give us the basis for a fine name for the fear associated with machines: *mechaphobia.* Mechaphobia that can be insidious is not just fictional. Among its potent effects, mechaphobia is a very real factor in the progress, or lack thereof, toward education on planet Earth. Today's most common form of educational mechaphobia is caused by digital technologies. There are frequent scenes in educational settings where people are seething as they deal with computers and eagerly wishing they could blow them up or douse them with acid. Granted, the emotion often is more than fear and includes justifiable anger at opaque instructions and inexplicable crashes, but these all need to be overcome and not used to justify ceasing to use the machines.

When computers began to appear in classrooms they were threatening simply because they were new. That is human nature. When the first military vehicles were introduced into the Army during the decade before World War I, the cavalry was horrified. They could not have imagined that the Jeep would be an officer's steed in World War II. When the Wright brothers got aviation off the ground in 1903, mechaphobes scoffed: *If God had meant us to fly, he would have given us wings.* This expression is such a telling one that it remains an aphorism today. A search for it on the Internet brought many versions. My favorites are Mel Brooks: *If God wanted us to fly, He would have given us tickets,* and George Winters: *If God had really intended men to fly, He'd make it easier to get to the airport.*[2] There is, of course, a darker side to opposing innovation. The cavalry soldier had to learn to drive. The skills and valor of the horseman were a proud tradition coming down through millennia of the annals of human conflict. All of this was to be replaced by a noisy, smoking, clanging tin can on wheels that got stuck in the mud and ran out of gasoline? The cavalry tradition did not die easily. One of the most memorable cartoons from World War II is Bill Mauldin's drawing of a heavyset sergeant standing with his back to his broken-down Jeep, his pistol pointed at the vehicle's hood, and his other hand covering his eyes. Mauldin took pride in what he captured, writing in his book *Up Front:* "It was a picture of an old-time cavalryman shooting his Jeep, which had a broken axle. It is one of those cartoon ideas you think up rarely; it has simplicity, it tells a story, it doesn't need words. It is, I believe, the very best kind of cartoon."[3]

The message the cartoon conveys about mechaphobia is an encouraging one: you can get over it. At some point the cavalry sergeant had gotten off of his horse and into his Jeep. He had learned how to use the pedals on the floor and the stick in his hand. He had exchanged reigns for a wheel. The machine had replaced his horse as his means of transportation. The days of the horse and buggy have become history. It would be hard to explain to anyone who drives a modern Jeep why anyone ever called a Schuttlerwagon like the beauty in figure 3.1 reliable.

One of the U.S. Cavalry's early adopters of motor vehicles was George S. Patton. When he graduated from West Point in 1909, young Patton chose to be assigned to the cavalry branch of the Army. He represented the United States in the 1912 Olympics in Stockholm. His event was the modern pentathlon, consisting of five events, including riding, that represented the skills of a military man. He finished an impressive fifth in the world. While he was in Europe, he studied sword drill at the French cavalry school.

All of Patton's biographers agree: his goal in life was to go to war. Pursuing that goal, in 1914 he unsuccessfully requested assignment to the French Cavalry. Instead of going to Europe, he ended up leading troops on horseback drills into the desert surrounding the Army cavalry post Fort Bliss, established in 1849 outside

Figure 3.1. *The Old Reliable Schuttlerwagon* 19th-century advertising card from Racine and Cortland Spring Wagon sold by the Emporia Hardware Co. of Emporia, Kansas

of El Paso, Texas. In 1916, the eager young cavalry officer saw his first military action as the U.S. Army chased Pancho Villa across the border into Mexico. Villa and his guerrillas had entered the United States and attacked Columbus, New Mexico, and its military outpost. Eighteen Americans were killed, including eight soldiers. Fort Bliss commandant General John Pershing was ordered to retaliate, and Lieutenant Patton went along as his aide. During an encounter, Patton used his revolver to kill the head of Villa's bodyguard and another Mexican fighter. This is the account of the expedition from Pershing's biography posted on the Web site of Arlington National Cemetery, where he is interred:

> On 15 March 1915, Pershing led an expedition into Mexico to capture Pancho Villa. This expedition was ill-equipped and hampered by a lack of supplies due to the breakdown of the Quartermaster Corps. Although there had been talk of war on the border for years, no steps had been taken to provide for the handling of supplies for an expedition. Despite this and other hindrances, such as the lack of aid from the former Mexican government, and their refusal to allow American troops to transport troops and supplies over their railroads, Pershing organized and commanded the Mexican Punitive Expedition, a combined armed force of 10,000 men that penetrated 350 miles into Mexico and routed Pancho Villa's revolutionaries, severely wounding the bandit himself. There is a prophetic photograph surviving from those days: a picture taken at Nogales of Generals Obregon, Villa and Pershing. Behind Pershing and to his left stands First Lieutenant George S. Patton, Jr.[4]

One of the other hindrances alluded to in this passage would produce mechaphobia in anyone being relied upon to achieve victory in the field. I have it on good authority that Pershing would happily have blown up his motor vehicles and poured acid upon their wrecks. My authority is my mother's father, Clarence Lupfer North, Sr. Born in 1882, Grandpa was three years younger than George Patton. As Grandpa used to put it when he told us about his involvement in the Villa affair, "General Pershing got stuck in the sand." He explained that the motor vehicles used by the Pershing expedition were some of the earliest ever put into service by the Army. In 1958 I wrote a college term paper about my grandfather, calling it "The Man with the Machinery." He had been involved in many technical aspects of the machines of his day in the desert southwest: trying to fix the water pumps into the flooding mines that were about to turn Tombstone, Arizona, into a ghost town; rigging buckets that hauled tons of bat guano out of Carlsbad Caverns; and, supplying equipment for the booming mining era in which he lived. At the time Pershing's frustration with his motor vehicles led him to call for help, Grandpa was working for a company called Mine and Smelter Supply. He wrote out notes, which I still have, to use when I interviewed him. This is what he jotted down to remind himself as we talked about his service to Pershing:

> Gen. Pershing was assigned to capture Villa who fled back down in Northern Mexico. At this time the U.S. Gov. started using autos & Gas Trucks. Gen Pershing was having a time to keep the units in repair. I was called to go to Columbus and see Gen Pershing, and suggest the tools & equipment to keep these autos & Trucks in Repair. The result was I recd an order from Gen Pershing for the M&S Co to furnish a complete shop. A complete shop was furnished and I supervised erecting a shop which pleased Gen Per very much.
>
> When our Gov. entered World War #1, Pershing was ordered to pull his troops from Mexico and was assigned to Europe etc.
>
> I was called by Pershing to go to Washington, com[missioned] as a major to develop the shops for over seas and here to maintain all transportation. A motor transport corps was formed, etc.

Grandpa was a nerd techie of 1916, who came to the rescue of mechaphobes in the quartermaster corps. He was performing the duties of today's tech-help customer service. The autos and trucks were primitive and people who knew how to take care of horses and Schuttlerwagons had few clues about servicing ball

Figure 3.2. Mine and Smelter Supply Co. El Paso office. Clarence North is seated, front right. Circa 1910.

bearings, crunching sand, or a truck with a dirt-filled carburetor. Thirty years later, Bill Mauldin could still get a laugh out of a cavalry sergeant putting his Jeep out of its misery with a bullet.

Patton was not one to stay stuck in the sand. I do not know if he met my grandfather but he must have been well aware of his commander's mecha frustrations. Obviously Grandpa's tech skills very much impressed Pershing because he gave him the responsibility for figuring out how to keep the entire U.S. Army on its wheels during World War I. My guess is that Patton, too, was impressed by the shop that could be set up in the field to keep motor vehicles in attack mode. It may have helped the young warrior to see a future in battle for the new kind of machines. Patton impressed Pershing during the Mexican campaign; the general promoted him to captain and took him to Europe. Patton asked for a combat command post and took over the brand-new U.S. Tank Corps. He got off of his horse and became a leading pioneer and innovator of armored vehicle warfare. Oddly, it was a motor vehicle that ultimately cost him his life in December 1945. Not long after surviving a high-speed collision between his Jeep and an oxcart, he was killed in another accident as he was being driven in his 1938 Cadillac.

The handsome machine was a seven-passenger Fleetwood that had been delivered to France before the war, captured by the invading Germans, abandoned in their retreat, and commandeered by Patton for his use as a leader of the Allied occupation. Patton, they say, was at something of a loss about what he could do in private life after the war. He commented often that the proper end for the professional soldier is a quick death inflicted by the last bullet of the last battle. Perhaps he would feel that he died in the sort of saddle he had chosen for himself.

Mechaphobia is very useful for inexperienced teenage drivers and risk-taking generals. With motor transportation, it is fear of bodily harm. Mechaphobia has proven very common when it comes to trying to get people to use computers in the field of education because other sorts of fears are aroused. Before we take a look at the real or perceived causes for the fears of machines in education, let me make it clear that it is neither the spirit nor purpose of this book to dismiss mechaphobia. It is fascinating and, like all fears, may have its uses. What I will try to show you is that mechaphobia is barely relevant and basically insignificant in light of the benefits that will be delivered for the human mind through the lodging of our human ideas in the newly interconnected and rich digital media. But first, let us take a look at how mechaphobia has been affecting education.

Where would Western civilization be today if General John Pershing had left his mechas stuck in the sand and kept his troops on horseback? Indeed, he might have captured Villa by sticking to the old ways, but he was not one to look backward. When World War I started, he was made the commander of U.S. armed forces. He sent to El Paso for the young techie who had dug him out and told him to keep the machines running. That part did not always go smoothly. When Grandpa invented the gas station—the idea of putting tanks of gasoline underground with pumps on the surface the trucks could pull up to—he tested the idea at a field in Maryland. A heavy rain soaked the ground and the tanks rose through the surface; I have seen photographs of the resulting huge cracks in the concrete where the trucks were supposed to park. But the Motor Transport Corps did its work well, with the support of a blue-ribbon civilian board that brought its expertise. Among the members was auto pioneer Walter Chrysler. My grandfather liked and admired Chrysler and bought and drove his company's cars for the rest of his life.

Pershing took the brilliant and eager Patton to Europe and put him in charge of making the tanks effective in battle. Pershing whipped the mechas into shape. If he had fought World War I only with cavalry, at the least George Patton would not have gained the experience that gave him and his nation its prowess in World War II armored warfare. Hitler had mechamania. His blitzkrieg was a "violent surprise offensive by massed air forces and mechanical ground forces in close co-ordination."[5] In World War I, Pershing and Patton laid important groundwork for the Second World War, which in significant part was won by the ability of the United States to build and use mechanized military transportation and weapons.

Is there a parallel pattern for the adoption and effective use of mechanization in 20th century education? Certainly there are patterns of change brought about by machinery in many happier areas than warfare. A century ago civilian auto-mobiles were just as stuck in the sand and mud as Pershing's autos and gasoline trucks were. Today the ability of vehicles to cover all terrains, the surfacing of roads, and the construction of the interstates leave us stuck only in the traffic. Mechanization has transformed the broad sweep of industries from agriculture to construction, to manufacturing, to communication, to all forms of transporta-tion. Many of the new ideas for machines were developed for weapons and war, later being adapted to peacetime uses.

The story is entirely different for education. Shooting and teaching—these are very different things. It is certainly true that we can build a machine that shoots people, but can we build a machine that teaches people? We can build machines that sow and reap, dig and lift, trim and rivet, write and talk, sail and fly. When it comes to a machine trying to teach, there is hesitancy. It takes a hu-man being to be a teacher, or maybe educational mechaphobia keeps us from try-ing hard enough. I have seen some of the brightest and most sophisticated peo-ple I know blow up and pour acid on the idea of machines replacing teachers.

While fear is a useful response that calls attention to danger, it is not a useful state of mind for planning. Anger and frustration are helpful in fueling motiva-tion, but not good things to feel when making decisions. I doubt that Pershing made the decision to send for a techie to set up a repair facility out of fear, anger, or frustration. He was thinking about the future. The purpose of this book is to raise issues that need thought and innovation toward building the new sort of education that is emerging in the 21st century. The project is a joyous one, in fe-licitous contrast to the undertakings forced on the Pershings and Pattons of the 20th century. But forced on us it is, with as much inevitability and urgency as the burgeoning blight of fascism was forced on our grandfathers. The first step in the process is to put educational mechaphobia in perspective and get beyond it.

For the kids, mechaphobia has never been a problem. They are the early adopters of the key tools for future learning: the Internet and wireless communication devices. Most students in school today have had a mouse in their hand since they were toddlers. I am very often challenged on this assumption by people who argue that it is just the rich and privileged children who have the tools and sophistication for the wireless age. The reality I find is that like radio, television, and portable music devices, digital communication has spread into deep recesses of disadvantage and distance. For several years I have spot-checked with school kids I have met in New York City, seldom finding one who did not have Internet access at home, at a friend or relative's house, or (less often) at school. Digital machines and kids have a relaxed rapport. One of the easiest parts of the global spread of Internet access devices will be their adoption by kids. The process for this adoption is tracked at EdClicks.com in the Mechaphile section. In short, the kids usually have a much better idea of what the machine is capable of than adults do, as the following encounter demonstrates:

I talked with a couple of typical knowledgeable mechaphile kids on a shining May afternoon in 2001. I had taken the 50th Street Manhattan crosstown bus to the edge of the Hudson River and gotten off at the stop next to the mammoth USS Intrepid aircraft carrier museum. My mission was to get in some practice with my new mini-DV digital video camcorder. The machine is very sweet, and trying out its features got me to musing about the elegant mechas engineered for imaging over the span of my experience. I still have the Nikon single-lens reflex that I bought in 1964 when it was the sweetest imaginable camera of that time. It never takes a bad picture. Legend is that during the Korean War, a decade before I acquired my Nikon, some *Life* magazine photographers lost their European-made lenses on the battlefield and had to make do with replacements that had been manufactured in Japan. When the *Life* labs in New York saw the quality of the images on the film shipped in from Korea, the Nikon era was born. It seems primitive now, but my top-of-the-line F6 did not have a built-in light meter because the technology was not yet available. I was then writing advertising copy at an ad agency in El Paso, Texas, in a job that included production of radio and television. During the 1960s, while we were recording television spots at the local stations, KTSM acquired exciting new machines that recorded video on tape, and before long took the thrilling step to capturing color television images. The first color camera in El Paso was enormous and crowded the studio, rolled around on big wheels, and had three large lens systems, one for each color it recorded.

To get ready to test my new camcorder, I walked from the bus to a bench in the shadow of the Intrepid, sat down and opened my pack. The strap attached horizontally to the right side of the camera was soon holding the machine against my open palm. My hands are small, yet there was no feeling of burden or intrusion. The mecha just nestled in, ready to perform. It can do everything my Nikon can, and does have an internal light meter—or rather a set of sophisticated light-measuring systems. It also does everything the behemoth color television camera I first saw could do, and more and better. It has an attached, hinged screen that can be used for both viewing while recording and for playback. It is a little production studio as well, with special-effects, dubbing, and editing capabilities. It does everything in digital zeroes and ones, a method that existed not at all when I learned the ropes of image processing.

I began trying out some of my new camera's features. A group of kids, all African American, trooped across the middle of my first shot and I tried out the feature that would capture a still image during a motion sequence. When the group had passed, I practiced zooming in and out on a smiling Japanese tourist posing for friends in front of a World War II tank. (Times have changed incredibly since I was the age of the children I had just been taping!) As I stopped the camera, two of the kids walked over and sat down next to me on the bench. They were discussing something, looked up at me, and asked me if I had something to write on. I found a pad of paper in my pack, and handed a piece of paper to one of them. The other one asked if he could have a piece, too, and I obliged. The second one said brightly, "You see, people really are nice." I pointed out that they were small pieces of paper and not a big deal.

By then they had seen my camera and gotten excited. "Can we be on TV?" they asked. They posed next to me on the bench, I aimed my machine at them, and we chatted as they were recorded. As we watched the playback of their images on the screen attached to the camera, they asked where the audio was. I didn't know, but one of them showed me where the volume button was and after I clicked it several times to raise the sound level, we could hear our voices.

I asked when school would be out and they gave me an exact date three weeks later. They told me they were graduating, because they were finishing the sixth grade. They said they attended a public junior high school in Brooklyn and were with their class for a visit to the Intrepid, where a relative of someone at school was employed. One of the kids took off, and I asked the other one if he made good grades. He looked a little sour and indicated they were not all that great. I asked him what he liked to study, and got even less of a response. The boy then tried to be polite by giving the sort of canned answers young people have for adults about their schools, "We have math and social studies." I asked him if he studied on the Internet. He was apologetic, saying that there was no computer at home, but they were going to get one fixed so he could use it in the fall. He then said he used the Internet sometimes at school. The shift in his mood when I asked him about his school is typical. The camera was exciting; school is not.

Clearly, the notion of putting machines into schools just because they are exciting to students and kids take to them with enthusiasm and mystifying competence is not a reason unto itself for making them part of education. The reason to put machines that access the Internet into the hands of students is the content that the machines will give them. We are not talking about a new kind of chalkboard; we are talking about a new environment for the intellect. In the case of my cameras, the machine changed, becoming smaller, sleeker, and more portable. Yet there is very little that can be done by my new camera that we could not do one way or another with the larger equipment we had in El Paso in the 1960s. The camera is a newer machine but it delivers no *deus*. In many industries, digital machines, like my digital camera, have come along over time to perform tasks that were once done by mechanical devices or people. There is no comparable history in education. There were no machines in the classrooms of any decade in the 20th century that performed in new ways the core thrust of education: to provide learning. While the technology of the 20th century came to play a dominant role in a spectrum of human activity, from agriculture and transportation to media and war, it did not catch on to any significant degree in the aspects of education that involved learning. Ditto machines have been replaced by word processors and administrative connectivity has increased where schools are wired. But machinery has not taken a significant role in the pedagogy—in leading students to knowledge. A Xerox does the same copying job as the ditto machine, only better—but a chalkboard replaced by Internet access is a paradigm shift. The Internet is not only a new method, but it does something that was impossible before it emerged.

The strain of mechaphobia that makes a lot of us dyspeptic and vitriolic when we think about a machine replacing a human teacher has been incubating for a long time. Technology in pedagogy has an array of critics. A leading one, Larry Cuban, tracked the hails and farewells issued over the decades to 20th-century classroom technical panaceas. He concluded in 1986 that "the search for improving classroom productivity through technological innovations has yielded very modest changes in teacher practice without any clear demonstration that instruction is any more effective or productive after the introduction of radio, films, instructional television, or computers."[6] More telling than the educational insignificance of the media Cuban mentioned is the deep-rooted article of faith that the teacher must be human. More than faith, the necessity of a human teacher may be the practical explanation for the failure of machines to assume a larger role in the classroom. And even if machines could implant knowledge into inquiring minds, it concerns us that children would lose the nurture and inspiration of a human teacher. Machines in education seem to threaten the teacher's role and the teacher's job security.

We need to be very thoughtful if we feel an attack of educational mechaphobia coming on. Just exactly what are we afraid of? There are teaching machines that are very effective and very important, like flight simulators. I once got to sit in the back seat of one of them while my nephew, then a high school student enamored of flying, made a simulated landing in New Jersey. It happened at training facility where several simulators perch on elaborate metal legs anchored to the floor of a large trench. The box containing a mock cockpit is entered across a walkway from the side of the room housing the big teaching machines. The scene is a bit comical when you watch a simulator in use from the outside. It wiggles, tips, and bumps atop its legs. But when you are inside, the illusion is complete that you are riding in the cockpit of an airliner. The machine is able to simulate real flight and to teach the pilot what will happen under a wide variety of circumstances. The fact that the machine can teach does not give me mechaphobia—rather I would be afraid to fly in an aircraft where the pilot had not learned from the requisite hours in a simulator now routine for commercial pilots. We learned on 11 September 2001 just how effective the flight simulator mecha can be in teaching a student how to handle an aircraft.

The scene in *A.I.* where the people are acting out their hatred of machines in the Flesh Fair reveals malice hard to imagine toward mechanical things that were inferior to humans. The real problem must be that fear of the superior aspects of the machines, where they could do things better than people could. But does that make any sense when it comes to machines teaching? Or is there fear that human teachers will lose their jobs and status if the machines take over some aspect of their roles? The fact of the matter is that machines have been part of teaching at least since the abacus was invented thousands of years ago. The abacus, like many fine software tutorials, is a useful machine for gaining practice in mental calculation. Although the abacus does not do any calculations, as later mathematical machines do, it provides visualization to supplement memory and display aspects of the problem under way while its human being does mental calculations.

My nephew who did the simulated landing in New Jersey is now a professional pilot. I asked him recently about how the simulators are used and he put his finger on the key factor in choosing a machine as the teacher. He pointed out, "You can teach all kinds of different scenarios in a simulator that you could never do in a real aircraft." A book or a classroom setting could not teach as well that simulated landing in New Jersey. The cockpit visual experience, the sense of motion, and the responses to the pilot's good and false moves are immediate, graphic, and kinetic in the simulator. If the pilot in training faced a crisis like the one my inattention caused when I almost crashed my Jeep into the wall, the simulator will provide a safe pullout or a virtual crash depending on the reactions performed by the pilot. The simulator is a far better teacher than a human being for this training. It is also fair to say that the simulator is a nurturing and inspiring teacher, rewarding success and giving an aspiring pilot a strong measure of the thrill of flying—while safe in a tin can that stands on sturdy legs only a few feet above the ground. Perhaps software can be added to simulators to alert managers of training facilities to the possibility that someone using their simulators is practicing suspicious maneuvers, such as those who destroyed the World Trade Center may well have done in the simulators they used in their pilot training. Maybe the software has already been written.

By now you may be thinking of your third-grader inside a box with a kiosk that is teaching him how to do his fractions. If so, does that idea frighten you? Maybe it is better than the last learning episode he experienced concerning fractions at school, where he may have been bored or did not understand—or maybe he has never really been challenged to master fractions. At the least, in the months and years ahead very stimulating and exciting new options will be created for learning. Perhaps you are completely satisfied with the education you received, and with what you were able to locate and/or provide for your own children. But what about other people's children?

My initial acquaintance with teachers was under the very best of the conditions that existed in U.S. schools in the middle of the 20th century. The public schools that I attended in San Antonio, Austin, and Bastrop, Texas, during World War II and thereafter in El Paso offered excellent teachers. I have many personal memories of women who fit the idealized stereotypes of the sort of teachers people are afraid would be replaced by machines. Miss Gillette taught music classes that my fourth grade attended three times a week at Crockett School. She taught from the front of the classroom seated behind her piano upon which sat a meditating bust of Beethoven. Most of what I know about the strings, reeds, winds, and horns of orchestras I learned from her. Mrs. Burtis taught 7B English at Austin High School, the alma mater I share with Sandra Day O'Connor, and many other successful and distinguished former students, including John Clendennin who led Bell South into corporate prominence. Each time students walked in to begin Mrs. Burtis' class there were seven challenging new vocabulary words written on the board that soon kicked off rich exchanges among the students and with our teacher. The Crockett principal, Miss Swann, and the Austin principal, Mr. Appleby, were respected and admired by all of us in the schools. A half century later I can still name at least a dozen more wonderful teachers from my school days. I was lucky—or maybe a lot of students are. We did have some mechanical innovations but they had little to do with learning. For example, when I was a freshman at Austin, the public address system was installed, replacing the long, yellow sheet of announcements that had been distributed daily by runners to every classroom to be read aloud during homeroom period. There is a cause for some mechaphobia here, as the public-address interruptions of class time has become an issue that makes the good old days of paper bulletins seem not all that bad.

Over the past 20 years I have met many teachers and principals within the New York City public school system. From 1982–91 I coordinated a partnership program called MENTOR that paired law firms with public high schools and junior high schools. After the pilot program and a year of expansion in New York, the program began to be copied in other cities where I served as the liaison between the lawyers and teachers. There may be bad people teaching school, but I did not meet them. Instead, I became acquainted in every school I visited with dedicated and effective people like my own school teachers and principals.

I am convinced the most fundamental reason for the current education crisis and seemingly failing schools is not the kids, as the last chapter suggests. I do not think it is the teachers, either. Wonderful, gifted people are attracted to teaching on a steady basis, and leave on a steady basis. Most of the ones I worked with on the MENTOR program were superstars who managed to put their love and devotion to teaching above the frustrations. If we define *teacher* as one who is dedicated to leading students to learning something, the frustrations for today's teachers are monumental. The fundamental pain teachers suffer today is their inability to cause their students to learn. There are two broad, sweeping, and effective ways in which the Internet will provide new answers to this problem, and neither one replaces nor competes with human teachers. Mechaphobia wrongfully postpones the realization of this new fuel and new sort of engine for learning. The new fuel is the access to knowledge from the Internet. The new engine is the as-yet largely underdesigned and unproduced software and hardware that will virtually lead students to knowledge.

Before discussing these new engines further, it is important to allay any mechaphobia caused by fear that teachers will be replaced by machines. I think quite the opposite is true: the Internet as the knowledge resource for teaching will help stem the exodus from the profession. By providing both student and teacher access to knowledge, both are relieved from arduous nonlearning and nonteaching tasks of rounding up and presenting material to be learned. To the extent that teachers can be replaced by machines, as they are by the simulators used by pilots, the machines free the human teachers for other tasks like inspiration and Socratic discourse.

What lies ahead is not going to be simply education as it used to be, only with machines added on. It will not be like the change I remember from the 1940s when the inkpot and dipping pen disappeared from our grade school desks and we tried to contend with the first ballpoint pens (they leaked a lot and I have never learned to like them!). The change is not simply like replacing handwriting instruments and typewriters with word processors. Online education so far has been essentially the repositioning of established methods and materials into the Internet—and that is at best a primitive beginning. The real change will be when computers are used as the major source of knowledge and used to interface that knowledge in profoundly rich, new ways. That fact is another cause of mechaphobia. People who fear the machines because things will be different are most comfortable with repositioning instead of innovation. The term *repositioning* comes up frequently in the early phases of a new medium. The invention of photography, for example, led to the repositioning of portraits from canvas to tin, and then paper. When the new technology begins to work, the tech team naturally grabs the most obvious output from earlier media and repositions it into the new medium. It takes time and out-of-the-box thinking to begin to exploit new capacities of the new medium. Things settled in long ago with portraiture. A superior portrait painter is able to capture the sitter far more profoundly than all but the most exceptional photograph. Photography, on the other hand, is superior in recording passing moments like the wedding kiss and baby's first step.

We will not have to reposition the process that we have called education during the 20th century into the 21st. Could we ask for better news? Yet there will be changes that will abolish some cherished old ways and cause treasured turf to disappear. Textbooks may not be printed for much longer. That will be the end of an industry. Knowledge itself may no longer be chopped up by grade, age, and subject and packaged as educational materials for sale because the essence of the Internet is combination that generates context. Testing may move online where kids may be able to take tests on their own, excel on them, and then opt out of the lockstep grades now mandated in schools. Young people may spend more time apprenticing in the workplace than they do sitting in classrooms. These are disruptions in an education routine of which we are deeply weary—and under which kids like those I met by the Intrepid clearly suffer. Let us not be afraid.

In the 21st-century learning process, the bodies of knowledge for the study disciplines will be accessed by students through the Internet. This will free the gift of teaching to lavishly grace the lives of learners. The root of the educational frustrations of the 20th century may have been the teachers' burden of force-feeding knowledge by spoonfuls. When teachers ration discrete chunks of knowledge according to strict schedules and approved textbooks, the most the kid receives is what her teacher and assigned textbook contain and share. The folly of this process became more and more obvious as the quantity of knowledge and the speed of its change and growth outpaced what teachers could learn and textbooks could keep current. The Internet came along just in the nick of time and a better way is developing. Teaching will once again become pedagogy: leading learners to knowledge. Schools will become scenes of articulation, Socratic challenges, artistic development, and scientific inquiry.

Lurking around the skirts of educational mechaphobia are justifiable fears for their futures of people who denigrate education advancement to secure their own control. Tutelage can become a trap and foster dependence. The arrival of *deus ex machina* has already begun to free generations now in school to explore study disciplines on their own in magnificent Web sites with the latest on their subjects presented interactively in rich text and graphics. You can visit many samples at EdClicks.com. Immanuel Kant challenged us with this admonition and exhortation:

> Enlightenment is man's release from his self-incurred tutelage. Tutelage is man's inability to make use of his understanding without direction from another. Self-incurred is this tutelage when its cause lies not in lack of reason but in lack of resolution and courage to use it without direction from another. *Sapere ande!* Have courage to use your own reason!—that is the motto of enlightenment.[7]

The root meanings of *tutelage* are guardianship and mastery, which are not the same thing as teaching. Effective teaching does not even require knowing the students personally. A great teacher for me was Dr. James McBath, who taught me debate logic in less than 10 hours, as I related in chapter 2. I never saw him again and I doubt he gave me another thought. I caution that it is deeply shameful to fan mechaphobia to reserve tutelage over young people. The vision of tutelage by a machine could be conjured to frighten us about children interfacing with computers.

Another perversity twists things to our loss when the digital technologies are used only to reposition and perpetuate the intractability and isolation of 20th century schools. It is the narrowest possible understanding of school wiring to think of it merely as a method for keeping attendance and communicating with the principal's office. It is not much more visionary to see the computers in the classroom as word processors, places to use CDs that contain interactive lessons, and machines that administer tests and assess their results. There is nothing wrong with the mechanization of these activities, but they miss the big picture. Worse, their clumsiness and rapid obsolescence make mechaphobics out of school administrators and budgeters, and rightly so. A recent prestigious *School Technology and Readiness Report*[8] set out these five *Key Building Blocks for Student Achievement in the 21st Century:* (1) assessment, (2) alignment, (3) accountability, (4) access (meaning equity among all students), and (5) analysis. These are essentially all tools of tutelage. To the extent that they employ machines to measure and slot students into curricula, my mechaphobic hackles are aroused. More to the point, to the degree this kind of emphasis in the education discourse deflects understanding of the learning feast on the Internet, our children and all learners are deprived. Another alliteration of goals for education might be: algebra, archaeology, authors, and the histories of Africa, the Americas, and Asia.

The Web sites listed for this chapter on EdClicks.com will give you a chance to evaluate whether learning mechaphobia makes sense to you. While focus in education discourse related to computers is typically far from the major action that is going on with knowledge itself, an explosion of learning is erupting toward unheard of bounty on the Internet. Do not dally with pen and chalk. As a parent, teacher, or mentor, the following are not acceptable excuses: I do not know how to type, I do not understand computers. Those excuses simply tell the world that you are mechaphobic. An excellent cure: next time you take a trip somewhere, ride a horse. It is too late to be an early adopter. You still have time not to be left in the dust. You will find that you feel much better when you are healed into mechaphilia, and you will discover that you are back in touch with kids. I urge you to join the thrilling collaboration that is forming the golden era of learning. I hope this book will encourage you to do that and give you some practical and visionary pointers.

The mecha that is now taking shape to complete the technical platform for 21st century learning is the handheld wireless device that is able to fully receive and interface the Internet. Its precursors are today's cell phones that are rapidly promising to reach the hands of just about every person on Earth. A set of diverse developments contribute to the promise that these devices will mature into full Internet platforms: hardware innovations, data compression, progress in beaming sophistication, enrichment, and sophistication of knowledge content, and the downward price in each of these sectors. The handheld wireless device that students will use will be small enough to slip into a large pocket and cheap enough to throw away. Schoolwork will be stored on a server somewhere on the Internet so that it is not device dependent. Software will also be obtained from the Internet so a girl in Morocco or Beijing can download worksheets in Arabic or Cantonese. Solar and/or rechargeable batteries will provide power and the Internet will be beamed to every location on the planet, making kids in the high mountains of Afghanistan and Peru or the deep jungles of Cambodia and Kenya able to learn without the geographical limits that have withered their educational opportunities in the past.

The title of the EdClick.com Web site refers to several ways education will click in the 21st century. The ubiquitous computers will be driven by incessant mouse and keyboard clicks as learning occurs from the Internet. Clicking up and down of buttons both mechanical and virtual on wireless devices will carry study disciplines to the farthest reaches of our planet and into the deepest recesses of ignorance and

Figure 3.3.   Education Clicking.

tyranny. The kids in school today are the leading sophisticates with the digital machines and already click away through thousands of Web pages that capture knowledge released by Pandora. The most fundamental click at the soul of education is the turning on of individual minds, which has begun and is accelerating.

The boys who showed me how to turn up the volume on my camera still must spend most of their school days in an imposed tutelage being drilled on spoonfuls of facts. Not a lot is expected of them at school from these fading aspects of 20th century education. You can look at Web sites collected at Ed-Clicks.com to see that the experience of students is of a different sort when they explore there, where they can freely acquire ideas and information to satiate their natural appetites. Will they do that? Kant says they should acquire the ability to make use of what they learn without direction from another. If you are a teacher, a key aspect of your responsibility is to guide students into self-tutelage. I believe that the Internet is quickly and magnificently opening to all children the full reservoir of human knowledge so that they may learn it. This wonderful change is causing the return of teaching to its fundamental purpose of liberating learners by showing them how to make their own use of what they learn—to be enlightened.

Looking at the lowest sort of expectations, the news is all good in the most practical sense. Every child today, even in the finest schools, is limited by geography and physical assets in what he or she may learn. An overwhelming majority of children across the planet have few books or other study resources. Their teachers may know little more than those who popped in and out of Abraham Lincoln's childhood. In our information age, even the most well-educated and best-informed teachers are hard put to stay up-to-date enough in their fields to enable them to serve as the repository of knowledge for their students. No high school biology teacher can hope to compete as a resource on the human genome with the online reports of *Nature* and *Science* magazines. It is false, except in the case of a few of the most well-versed of specialists, to expect the teacher to be the source of the knowledge; more appropriate sources are books and libraries. Socrates, Plato, and Aristotle surely expected their students to have read and absorbed knowledge from their books and those of others. This freed the classic masters to wrestle with ideas and help students become guardians of their own minds. I describe how I believe the schools of the future will return to the spirit of the classical academics, and go further then, ascending into new heights of the forming Internet common cloud.

But we need to first look at the education scene at the beginning of the 21st century from another perspective. Having confronted the hazards of mechaphobia, it is instructive to dip into today's golden swamp.

NOTES

1. A. O. Scott, "Do Androids Long for Mom?" *New York Times on the Web,* review of the movie *A.I.,* www.nytimes.com/2001/06/29/arts/29ARTI.html?pagewanted=print [accessed 30 June 2001].

2. *Great Aviation Quotes: Humor and Flying Jokes,* www.skygod.com/quotes/jokes. html [accessed 1 July 2001].

3. Bill Mauldin, *Up Front* (New York: Henry Holt, 1945), 113.

4. "John J. 'Black Jack' Pershing," Arlington National Cemetery Web site, www. arlingtoncemetery.com/johnjose.htm [accessed 1 July 2001].

5. *Merriam-Webster's Collegiate Dictionary,* 10th ed. (Springfield, Mass: Merriam-Webster, 1997).

6. Larry Cuban, *Teachers and Machines: The Classroom Use of Technology Since 1920* (New York: Teachers College Press, 1986), 109.

7. Immanuel Kant, "What Is Enlightenment?" in *The Art of Art History: A Critical Anthology,* ed. Donald Preziosi (New York: Oxford University Press, 1998), 70.

8. The CEO Forum, "Year 4 Star Report," www.ceoforum.org/reports.cfm [accessed June 2001].

4

THE PRIMORDIAL
INTELLECTUAL
INTERNET

The Golden Swamp

From the spot by the Hudson where I chatted with the two Brooklyn sixth-graders there is a clear view across the broad river. Taking in that view on 13 September 1609, we would have seen the first European ship to navigate those waters sailing by, square and lateen sails billowing from three masts of the 85-foot craft. The visitor was the Dutch ship Halve Maen (Half Moon), captained by Henry Hudson and crewed by 20 Dutch and English sailors. Apparently the ship was spotted by residents of Manhattan Island, because when it returned from its upper river explorations on 2 October, some of the Native Americans were hostile and Hudson ordered the ship's guns fired at them—crackling the air with the first gunshots to be heard on the island. The Half Moon left New York Harbor on 4 October and returned to Europe. A trickle of river traffic ensued from 1615, when the Dutch established Fort Orange on Castle Island near Albany, New York, as a post for trading furs with the Indians. In 1626, Peter Minuit purchased Manhattan from the natives and people from Europe have been docking and moving there ever since.

A variety of roles beckoned those drawn to the New World. Henry Hudson was an explorer. Peter Minuit was a merchant, serving as director general of the Dutch West India Company. People followed, performing different functions in winning the new land, making it productive, and finding both new paths and dead ends: soldiers, farmers, preachers and their flocks, tradesmen, artists, thieves, adventurers, slaves, and teachers. The Internet world has been occupied in a similar manner. It began as an arena of exchange for science and other academic subjects. Opportunities it offered when the World Wide Web and its browsers opened the cyber frontier have been grabbed and exploited. For education, many have commented that the impact of the Internet is much like that of the invention of the printing press. When Johann Gutenberg figured out how to use movable type to produce reading material, books could be mass produced and knowledge was allowed to spread beyond the elite and over great distances. Abraham Lincoln was a beneficiary, and through him an entire nation was as well, in his leadership for the preservation of the Union and the emancipation of the country's slaves. The Internet does also achieve broader access to ideas and information. But breadth is only one of several fundamental changes it is causing in how humankind will interface with what it knows in the future. Among these, a modification at least as major as individual access is the capacity for universal sharing of the same knowledge resource. The Internet provided Pandora with a medium into which to turn loose everything known. The web structure and nodes of the Internet offer a radically new way to consolidate the most valid facts and ideas, keep them up-to-date, and let them be studied by anyone and everyone on the planet. A young Lincoln today need not get his Latin from an itinerate "wizzard" who may teach him incorrectly; he can study Latin virtually online and move through related literature and history.

Before the benefits of access and shared resources can have significant effect, the world first needs to figure out how to find what is out there. The first step in doing so was the theme of the last chapter: Do not be afraid of the technology; master the machines; put your horse out to pasture and get behind the wheel. Once you do that, you will discover the next difficulty. You will feel a great deal like General Pershing did when he turned loose his trucks to chase Pancho Villa. With a switch of metaphor, I predict you will not find yourself stuck in the sand, but will have plunged into a swamp. The waters will be muddy and some strange and ugly things will float by. Do not be frightened. Grab onto the happy thought that although it may be a swamp, the Internet is a golden one for education. Things are rapidly getting better, and some investigation of the nature of the swamp and why it is golden is illuminated by comparing it to a swamp of another era.

In many ways, the Internet of the beginning of the 21st century is parallel in energy and intellectual vigor to the city that funded Henry Hudson's first European voyage up the Hudson River. The Internet environment is radically different from other media previously used by our species to exchange and store what we know. That new environment is closest in similarity to our brains, but brains are infinitely more advanced. The Internet is not like a brick-and-mortar library, which consists of shelves of discrete volumes of data and ideas arranged by subject and author. The Internet does not work like broadcast media that roll out words and images in time. Knowledge nuggets within the Internet behave more like the golden cans linked together here and there and floating in the swamp in figure 1.1 of this book. The undeveloped and developing intellectual Internet is also very much like Holland once was in several striking ways.

Civilizations are nurtured by abundant water. Egypt sat upon the sands along the beneficent Nile River that helpfully watered crops periodically and always flowed by for irrigation and transportation. Agriculture required little effort and minds, backs, and hands engaged in formulating designs, erecting great monuments, and jotting things down in increasingly sophisticated pictographs. The Mayans of Central America enjoyed a home where, because it rained a lot, the jungle was bountiful, and there was plenty of time to carve intricate designs in stone. The Tigris and Euphrates rivers, and to the east, the Indus and the Yellow and Yangzi, watered the birthing of early civilizations. Civilized progress was very slow along the eastern shore of the North Sea where the problem was too much water. Until its residents began their all-out effort to conquer the waters about a thousand years ago, those Netherlands were barely habitable by humans. Wetland archaeology experts Bryony and John Coles described what its early peoples had to deal with:

> Their world was one of water, vegetated water, broken by the sinuous lines of the raised banks that followed rivers and creeks. Tidal influence reached far inland, causing freshwater creeks to rise and fall by as much as a metre. The banks or levees that bounded the watercourses were covered with alder, and oak, and other deciduous trees on their drier parts. Behind them was more water, the back swamp, where reeds and other marsh vegetation might grow. Occasionally, a relic sand dune stood out, a rare island of sandy dry soils. Inland were great peatbogs cut by creeks and rivers; sea-

wards lay salt marshes and a narrow belt of coast sand dunes stood out. The systems of creeks, levees, and backwaters underwent many changes as the sea level fluctuated and wet phases were separated by phases of brushwood growth and peat formation.[1]

Two thousand years ago, Pliny wrote an eyewitness account of what life was like for the residents of what is now the mild and lovely Dutch landscape:

> I have myself personally witnessed the condition of the Chauci, both the Greater and the Lesser, situate in the regions of the far north. In these climates a vast tract of land, invaded twice each day and night by the overflowing waters of the ocean, opens a question that is eternally proposed to us by Nature, whether these regions are to be looked upon as belonging to the land, or whether as forming a portion of the sea?
>
> Here a wretched race is found, inhabiting either the more elevated spots of land, or else eminences artificially constructed, and of a height to which they know by experience that the highest tides will never reach. Here they pitch their cabins; and when the waves cover the surrounding country far and wide, like so many mariners on board ship are they; when, again, the tide recedes, their condition is that of so many shipwrecked men, and around their cottages they pursue the fishes as they make their escape with the receding tide.[2]

I am sure that in your experience, the islands of Internet quality can seem isolated and swamped like the few and scattered high spots of ancient Holland. The villages that grew to become the towns and cities of modern times originally perched on the *terpen* of the watery past. These mounds above the ancient water level, now called *terps* by archaeologists, were composed of turf, earth, charcoal, manure, and other debris.[3] It is a fact that we encounter some of the characteristics of turf, earth, charcoal, manure, and other debris piled up within the Internet swamp. How Holland rose from its water and debris to boast the most golden town on the globe is instructive.

By A.D. 1100, most of Europe had assumed a vital role in Western civilization. Even the Vikings, most distant of the Europeans from the Rome where all roads had led, had spent some generations in Normandy, conquered England, and left significant cultural legacies in several faraway places. In the 12th century, the Dutch were just beginning the battle in earnest that would tame their waters. The future central port of the emerging country was starting to grow on a spot of land next to a dam on the Amstel River. As the 13th century began, the lord sovereign had declared Amsterdam to be a juridical town. Enjoying a modest economy based on beer and herring, the town grew slowly over the next two centuries, expanding from its center by the dam. Making the town bigger involved filling land and digging canals. In the 15th century, Amsterdam became part of the Burgundian Empire, emerged as an important harbor for Holland's fish and grain, and was soon the country's largest city, boasting 30,000 residents. By the 17th century, Amsterdam was one of the finest cities in Europe. Here is a description of how the Dutch managed to erect a great city on a location that Pliny and others suspected really belonged in the watery realm:

> This metropolis was built on land seemingly least propitious for its development—the marshes formed at the mouth of the Amstel in the Ij's inlet. The original cluster of structures was raised on a few strips of land projecting at right angles into the river's mouth. Later, this nucleus of a town was enveloped by a semicircular canal, the *Singel* 'Belt.' The builders were constructing upon sodden land which invariably revealed water at a depth of a few feet everywhere they dug. For this reason, all the houses of Amsterdam were built on pilings made of long, stout beams in trestle form driven into the spongy soil and taking the place of ordinary foundations. Hence the ironical popular verse of the time:

> The great town of Amsterdam
> Is built on piles, until
> The day the whole place tumbles down:
> Then who will pay the bill?[4]

The forces that combined to release the energy and prosperity that raised the tall houses atop deep-driven piles along Amsterdam's canals caused a sweet spot in time for the Dutch. One of Holland's most sophisticated sons was Constantijn Huygens, a diplomat and secretary to the Prince of Orange. In addition to his roles in public affairs, Huygens was a poet, composer, musician, and patron of the arts. The perceptive Dutchman dubbed Amsterdam the "golden swamp." For one thing, the city was very wealthy, profiting enormously from the Dutch East India Company headquartered there. Also based in the city was the Dutch West India Company that had underwritten the voyage in which Henry Hudson explored the river that bears his name. Many other forms of trade and commerce flourished. Although Huygens probably was thinking of money when he coined the phrase, Amsterdam and the Holland of that day were golden in other ways as well.

Toleration was a deeply held principle for the Dutch, having struggled against religious persecution under Spanish domination whose ending helped usher in Holland's golden age. In cosmopolitan Amsterdam on a 17th century Sunday church services were held by Calvinists, Remonstrants, Lutherans, Mennonites, and Catholics. High German and Portuguese Jews gathered in their synagogues on Saturdays. Those who came to Holland to practice their faiths freely included Jews, Calvinist protestants from France and Germany, and a growing stream of English Separatists. One group of the Separatists arrived in Amsterdam in 1608 and moved to Leiden the next year. In 1620, intent on sailing for America, they bought the ship *Speedwell* in Leiden and sailed to England. The *Speedwell* leaked alarmingly, prompting the pilgrims to purchase the *Mayflower* in England, from where they sailed to found the Plymouth colony in Massachusetts. Pilgrim leader William Bradford recorded the experience of the Separatists in Holland. He wrote this description in 1609:

> For these & some other reasons they removed to Leyden, a fair & bewtifull citie, and of a sweete situation, but made more famous by ye universitie wherwith it is adorned, in which of late had been so many learned man. But wanting that traffike by sea which Amerstdam injoyes, it was not so beneficiall for their outward means of living & estats. But being now hear pitchet they fell to such trads & imployments as they best could; valewing peace & their spirituall comforte above any other riches whatsoever. And at lenght they came to raise a competente & comforteable living, but with hard and continuall labor.[5]

As Bradford's reference to the "universitie" suggests, intellectual tolerance and freedom were another glowing facet of Holland's golden age. After three decades of study and travel, Frenchman Rene Descartes chose Holland as his permanent home in 1629. The decision was well thought out and apparently a good one; the mathematician-philosopher stayed for the next 20 years and produced the work which brought him fame. Descartes said he liked Amsterdam because you can buy anything you want, you are free, and you are safe.[6] From Holland, Descartes stayed in touch with other scientists and thinkers including Marin Mersenne and Claude Mydorge in France and Dutchman Christiaan Huygens—the only son of Constantijn Huygens. Certainly as a parent the senior Huygens could relish his son's intellectual stature and accredit Amsterdam for the golden opportunities Christiaan had to learn.

Figure 4.1.   This image of Amsterdam is derived from the eyes and hand of Rembrandt when the city was the golden swamp. Posterizing and cutout digital filters were applied, combining some of the tiny lines of his etching tool.

Three years after Descartes relocated to Holland, Amsterdam gave birth to philosopher Baruch Spinoza. His family were Jews who had fled persecution in Portugal. Baruch grew up in the golden swamp and was trained in the Talmudic tradition. His thinking swerved from the conventional. His community feared his views would bring persecution upon them and Spinoza was offered 1000 florins to keep quiet. He refused, and at the age of 24 he was excommunicated by a rabbinical court. The remainder of his life he supported himself grinding lenses, remaining in Holland and there creating his philosophy and written works. He died in 1677 at the Hague.

Born the same year as Baruch Spinoza, in 1632 in Delft, Antoni van Leeuwenhoek grew into an inquiring scientific layman and broke the barrier into the invisible world by building microscopes. He was an unlikely fellow to be expected to become a major contributor to biology. A tradesman from a family of tradesmen, he had no special education and spoke only Dutch, limiting his ability to communicate within the scientific world. He described his motivation and experience in a letter in June 1716:

My work, which I've done for a long time, was not pursued in order to gain the praise I now enjoy, but chiefly from a craving after knowledge, which I notice resides in me more than in most other men. And therewithal, whenever I found out anything remarkable, I have thought it my duty to put down my discovery on paper, so that all ingenious people might be informed thereof.[7]

What stimulated van Leeuwenhoek's craving after knowledge? Was it the golden swamp of Holland into which he was born? If so, that same swamp mist may have affected Spinoza's creativity and attracted Descartes to settle down. I believe that a golden era of learning is dawning now because from the golden swamp that is the Internet seeps and steams that same marvelous mist that wakens creativity and intellectual craving. The vapors of knowledge are billowed by knowing. Knowledge begets knowledge. Knowing becomes an end unto itself. For sure Antoni van Leeuwenhoek thought so.

We must not leave the discussion of golden swamp genius without mentioning the artists. One of them, Johannes Vermeer, was also born in 1632 and in the same month and town as van Leeuwenhoek. Both men lived out their lives in their native Delft. Any collaboration by them is unknown, but Vermeer's interest in optics is well established. Vermeer used a camera obscura, as did Constantijn Huygens; Huygens knew both van Leeuwenhoek and Vermeer.

The giant among the Dutch artists of the day was arguably the greatest painter of all time: the quintessential golden age Dutchman Rembrandt van Rijn. We look in on him first in the 1620s before he moved to Amsterdam. He is still in his family's hometown of Leiden, working with his partner, Jan Lievens. Constantijn Huygens had visited the two young geniuses and lamented: "They are rather full of themselves and have not yet deemed it necessary to devote a few months to a study visit to Italy. . . . How I would love them to become acquainted with the likes of Raphael and Michelangelo and to make the effort to draw inspiration from the creations of so many towering geniuses!"[8] Huygens was concerned for the young men because the grand tour to Italy was considered a must if a young painter were to have real hope of making the big time.

Anthony Bailey, who recaptures historical Holland in several wonderful books, explains that in the golden swamp of Rembrandt's day it was not the young painter's ego that kept him from using crucial months of development to sojourn to Italy:

> Rembrandt had said he was too busy to go—and besides, he could see all the Italian art he wanted here in Holland. His teacher Pieter Lastman had passed on to him (and to Lievens) some of the Italianate fashion, and there were others in town whose work could be seen, influenced by a stay in Italy, by the Italian light, by the classical and the antique, and by the paintings of Caravaggio and Adam Elsheimer, a German who spent the last ten years of his life in Rome. The Grand Tour, as made by John Evelyn

or young Jan de Witt, who was to become Holland's leading statesman in the latter part of Rembrandt's life, could be made—as far as the painter was concerned—within walking distance of the Breestraat.[9]

Although the young Rembrandt could not go online, as students can today, to study art from throughout the world on his desktop, he could take a short walk to view virtually all of the visual ideas and influential images of his day.

The Dutch golden swamp power elite were not the politicians, clergy, artists, or intellectuals. The authority and respect for running things belonged to the merchants. Gaspard van Barlaeus, a professor of philosophy and theology in Leiden and Amsterdam over the first half of the 17th century, held up the ideal to his countrymen of the *mercator sapien*—the wise merchant. Commerce drenched the swamp in money, putting gold in your pocket in a wonderful place where you could buy anything you wanted, as Rene Descartes said.

The first comparison of the Holland we have been describing and the Internet at the beginning of the 21st century is that they are both swamps. The word *swamp* is a very stimulating one for most of our imaginations, conjuring many pictures. One from my childhood in East Texas still would keep me from sticking a hand or foot into swamp water: there might be a water moccasin snake lurking in the murk who could bite me. I also heard talk back then of visiting swamps at night, taking along a flashlight to shine on the black water to attract frogs, and then sticking them: yuk! There was never a possibility that I would go along on such a sortie. Swamps I have in my mind's eye are full of mosquito larvae that hatch into aerial attackers who make red spots and carry disease. The Internet swamp is also abounding in junk, including figurative frogs, and contains its serious hazards. The list of what composed the ancient Dutch terps scattered though cyberspace is virtually on point: turf, earth, charcoal, manure, and other debris. Internet parlance could be: excess proprietorship, dirt, burned down sites, porn, and useless pages. The influx of all that stuff has stifled the surfing pleasures once enjoyed on the infant Internet, glutted the text-search spiders, and cultivates a widely accepted view that chaos cripples any useful big picture of cyberspace.

Everything, of course, was also able to pour into Amsterdam and flow out on canals through Holland, as ships from throughout the world docked in the harbor. History tells us that the free flow of goods and ideas led not to chaos and debauchery, but to material prosperity and intellectual achievement and vision.

Their muddy past must have made them tidy in prosperity, shedding wooden shoes on the doorstep so as not to track mud inside. I believe the same future is unfolding for the Internet because wise merchants and intellectual visionaries have taken the Internet plunge into the teeming swamp—and if you are one of them, you can help. At Amsterdam, along with the commerce and immigration, the coming together of what was known fed thought. That helps us understand why Descartes evaluated the rest of Europe and settled in Amsterdam.

It is probably no longer possible to make significant contributions to the future of learning if you do not realize that the raw knowledge material has now primarily cascaded into the Internet. The Internet is not a secondary or adjunct research tool, it has become the first and foremost tool. A very great deal has happened since Pandora started lifting the lids of knowledge repositories less than 10 years ago. Like the cargoes of ships grand and small tying up along Amsterdam's docks and canals, unloading people and wares from distant ports, the pure gold of human knowledge has flowed into the Internet to create the fantastic new cyber biome of ideas. The Internet is today a glorious and golden swamp. The immediate challenge is to navigate the swamp, but we should refine the gold as well. In chapters that follow I will suggest ways we can, as did the Dutch, rescue from the swampy terrain a parkland and fair graced by pavilions—doing so is the happy enterprise of creating tomorrow's learning environment.

The increasing availability of things to learn on the Internet parallels, with a disquieting irony, the decreasing achievement by students in public schools and the growing removal by parents of their children to alternative schools and home-schooling. At least for some public school folk, the Internet looms as a threat to their turf, to use a modern meaning for what in Dutch terps was a more innocent mass of twisted roots, grass, and soil. This book is not about the education wars of territory and theory. My thesis is that one single factor will underlie how we will learn in the 21st century. The education wars raged throughout the 20th century, and a towering figure through it all was John Dewey. In the following passage from Diane Ravitch's history of the failure of schools in the 20th century, Dewey gives us a definition of the factor that is the subject of this book: "the organizing bodies of truth that we call studies." As you will see, Dewey did see a key importance of the *studies,* and Dr. Ravitch explains their bumpy fate:

> [John Dewey said:] "The child and the curriculum are simply two limits which define a single process. Just as two points define a straight line, so the present

standpoint of the child and the facts and truths of studies define instruction. It is a continuous reconstruction, moving from the child's present experience out into that represented by the organizing bodies of truth that we call studies."

The various school studies, such as arithmetic, geography, language, and botany, said Dewey, "are themselves experience—they are that of the race. They embody the cumulative outcome of the efforts, the strivings, and successes of the human race generation after generation. They present this, not as a mere accumulation, not as a miscellaneous heap of separate bits or experience, but in some organized and systematized way." Unfortunately, many of Dewey's disciples treated subject matter as an outmoded relic from an antediluvian past. Over the years, Dewey was far too tolerant of fellow progressives who adored children but abhorred subject matter.[10]

My goal is not to take a side in the not-so-golden swamp of curriculum debates, but it helps to realize that there are many opinions and definitions. In his basic text on the subject, *Curriculum Essentials*,[11] Jon Wiles sets out four definitions of *curriculum*, each supported by quotations from leaders in the field. The definitions are: curriculum as (1) subject matter, (2) a plan, (3) an experience, and (4) an outcome. It is my observation that as the computers have burgeoned, educators have grappled mainly with how to manage the last three definitions with digitally produced curricula forms (along with assessment, accountability, and other administrative stuff) while subject matter has been freed by Pandora and has settled happily into the Internet. Dewey noticed subject matter as *organizing bodies of truth*, and these very same studies are organizing more elegantly than ever within the new digital cyber medium, coloring the Internet into a golden swamp. Not confined to a Dutch harbor and the small nation it served, the Internet golden swamp is global. Just as surely as the Dutch sailed across the Atlantic and occupied Lower Manhattan, the French dotted the Mississippi, the Spanish marched through Mexico, and the English flowed into New England, and each penetrated from ports in Africa, Asia, and ocean islands—so have the sciences, arts, humanities, languages, technologies, and other study disciplines occupied the Internet. The escape of the study disciplines when Pandora opened the pot has forever changed where education will have to go to find them. They can never be returned to their previous vessels.

The metaphor of the golden age of Holland is the most exhilarating in pondering our global intellectual fate when we look at why historians call an era golden. Constantijn Huygens meant wealth when he dubbed Amsterdam a golden swamp. Historians have in mind art, literature, philosophy, liberty, and other cultural achievements when they bestow the golden label upon an age in history. On the wealth point, it is intriguing to realize that commerce caused the swamp of Amsterdam to be flooded with gold, as e-commerce may yet do with the Internet. More intriguing is this fundamental question: What is the swamp mist that caused the originality of the giants we have discussed? Why did the son of five generations of contented millers who ground grain adjacent to the Rijn River, and whose ancestors had focused for thousands of years on dealing with swamps—become, in the 17th century, the most original painter in history? In an ancient golden age, Plato observed that the Greeks had settled on the shores of the Mediterranean like frogs around a pond. The queen city of these frogs was Athens, where commerce and freedom spawned tidal waves of intellectual achievement that still toss and ripple our intellectual sea. How wonderful to think that the Internet is becoming a new mother of waters for learning and thought, with swamp mist rising to enthuse genius!

It cannot be a coincidence that Rembrandt's tiny country produced and attracted a cluster of contemporary originals. Several factors were at work then and are now characteristics of the Internet: the confluence and availability of ideas and knowledge; the rapidly increasing access to it by everyone; and the free exchange of thoughts among an unrestricted pool of the knowledgeable. A lens-grinder gave us microbiology! If the giants of the Dutch golden age showed us nothing else, they demonstrated that the exposure to inspiration and the ideas of others leads not to plagiarism but to originality. To stretch beyond the heights achieved by others, it helps to stand on their shoulders. The swamp mist that energized the originality of the 17th century Dutch was a concoction that included access to knowledge, the freedom to pursue it, and the synergy of relationships with other thinkers. Each of these are inherent in the Internet, and more ingredients will add to the mix. Again, you can help with that; there is a Swamp Mist section in EdClicks.com.

A bright promise for the golden age of learning that lies ahead is that it will make things different for other people's children. That, too, happened in 17th century Amsterdam. One of the most charming of Rembrandt's paintings is known as *Titus at His Desk*. Titus was Rembrandt's only child to survive to grow up into school age and he most certainly received the devotion of his father. Looking to be about 11 years old in the painting, Titus is leaning on his right hand, which contains a writing instrument, and is peering out of the picture, having looked up from a pile of papers. Although Titus would have been about 15 in 1655 when his father painted this portrait of him, he looks much younger, suggesting Rembrandt's fond memories of his little boy pausing from his studies to daydream. To replace the stack of papers with a wireless interface to the Internet will not replace the sort of experience young Titus had—it will amplify the richness of it manyfold.

Figure 4.2. *Beggars Receiving Alms at a Door*
The image is taken from a Rembrandt etching and has been altered with posterizing and cutout digital filters.

Rembrandt also drew other people's children; some are depicted in the image digitized from his etching of beggars in figure 4.2. The children of the golden swamp of 17th century Holland shocked the rest of Europe. Both boys and girls attended schools that were usually operated by a proprietor or a church and took place in a single room that was part of a residence or shop building, or in a barn. Curriculum was limited, the school operators who did the teaching were often incompetent, conditions were uncomfortable, and the kids were basically out of control. When they were not in school, things were worse. A scholar of the era, Paul Zumthor, describes the behavior of the Dutch kids:

> Until they were old enough to go to school the children mostly played in the street; if the family was rich the children were sent outdoors, unless the weather made this absolutely impossible, so that they should not disturb the house's perfect cleanliness; if the family was poor the street was the only place for them to go. So the Dutch town swarmed from morning onwards with children from three to six years old, of all classes of society, mixed into a playing, yelling, fighting mass on the pavements, under the house-canopies, along the streets. After the schools closed in the afternoons they were joined by the older ones. This open-air education was an extraordinary phenomenon for the time in Europe. It astonished all visitors from other countries, more especially since it went hand in hand with an indiscipline and rowdyism about which everyone complained. The urchins were disrespectful towards adults, and people whose clothes seemed strange to the juvenile mob could expect to be jeered at in the street if, indeed, they were lucky enough not to have stones thrown at them. The mob would attack passers-by, hurl lumps of earth at them and scream insults. This state of things became so widespread that it verged on public scandal; in Zaandam in 1642, for instance, the Church Council complained to the local magistrates who resuscitated an old police regulation. But all to no avail.... Excessive tenderness made parents incurably weak. If a visitor were to suggest to them that it might be appropriate to combat certain faults, he would be answered with a pessimistic dictum such as: "Cutting off the nose spoils the face."[12]

Embracing their kids, as well as keeping spotless houses, may have been a lingering habit from the early Dutch whose material luxuries had been very few in a messy, watery world always near disappearing into the sea. It is more certain that the appreciation and exercise of freedom underlay the liberties taken by the little ones; discipline enforcement in schools is easy in tyrannical states. In any event, the practice of providing schools open to all classes and the inclusion of girls, along with excessive tenderness, add yet more warmth to the nature of the golden age Dutch. The level of learning attained by the majority of Dutch kids was not very high, but learning was not limited to the elite, although a few of the wealthiest families did retain a pedagogue as a private tutor to guide the studies of their children.

The main difficulty in educating the children of golden age Holland was neither the lack of good intentions nor the undisciplined behavior of the kids, the latter being at least in part an outgrowth of boredom and frustration during school time. The insurmountable obstacle was a lack of the presence of knowledge in the classroom to put into the hands and heads of the students. Hard-copy school resources were limited to the Bible, some wall charts for letters and the like, and few if any additional books at the infant schools, attended during a child's first three years, and at the junior schools attended into adolescence. There was virtually no central administration of these schools on either the local or statewide level. The teachers could seldom make up the deficit of knowledge because they usually knew very little. Certification as a schoolmaster or schoolmistress required declaration of support for the reformed faith, but "neither the applicant's degree of learning nor his morals were made an object of genuine examination. . . . It was not until 1655 that an edict finally required that candidates for the post of teacher should be able to write, read printed and manuscript characters, perform the four basic mathematical calculations, know hymn tunes and . . . possess a sound method of teaching."[13] Yet Professor Zumthor is able to begin his next paragraph following the words just quoted with this surprisingly positive summation: "Despite the gross deficiencies of the system, and the fact that the schoolmasters constituted one of the poorest professional categories, a certain basic education was spread fairly widely and the proportion of illiterates was far smaller in the Union [Holland] than anywhere else in Europe."[14] As William Bradford mentioned about Leiden, it was "made more famous by ye universitie wherwith it is adorned, in which of late had been so many learned man." With rowdyism rampant and schools offering minimal learning, the fine universities bloomed in the Dutch golden swamp.

Did you notice the similarity between the description Abraham Lincoln gave of the teachers he had in rural frontier Indiana and the bottom-line certification requirements prescribed for Dutch teachers? They taught Lincoln enough for him to successfully encounter and master knowledge on his own. The Dutch kids lived in a golden swamp, in which floated most of what was known by humankind. Although the standards for what would be learned in the schools were minimal, like Lincoln, children in Holland were exposed to knowledge through books. Dipping once again into Professor Zumthor's description of their daily life:

> The Dutch were avid readers. Books were widely circulated, and their use was not reserved for a few privileged people as was the case in most other European countries at that time. The illustrated edition of the poems of Cats, a relatively expensive book, had sold fifty thousand copies by 1655, a fantastic figure for that era. Reading aloud, usually accompanied by a commentary or discussion, was one of the regular features of family life. Books were bought, but each family also had its collection of books handed down from previous generations and read and reread with the same pleasure.[15]

Religion was central in 17th-century life and in Protestant Holland the Bible was read along with commentary. Dutch Catholics continued to read traditional works concerning the saints, and the Spinozas and other Jewish families shared rabbinical literature. A variety of other kinds of books were read, including the classics and romantic tales of chivalry. Authors often took liberties with the facts in books about popular science and travel, that were hot topics producing big sales and broad readership. Professor Zumthor notes these specifics: "Bontekoe's Journal of his voyage to the Far East, published in 1646, ran to fifty editions. The Amsterdam bookseller Commelin had tremendous success with a book he published in 1644 consisting of twenty-one accounts of voyages to the Indies."[16] The golden swamp had broad horizons and its children grew up in an exciting and stimulating intellectual environment. We have a happy lesson to remember from the fact that this environment was available not only to the Dutch elite, but to other people's children throughout the Netherlands.

Dutch children were cherished and experienced knowledge. Perhaps neither Abraham Lincoln nor the kids in Holland would have gotten hooked on reading without their rudimentary exposure to learning at school. Maybe skills such as reading, writing, and arithmetic should be taught to children as a first step, and their engagement with knowledge as a secondary one that they should come to manage for themselves or in apprenticed activities. The lockstep march through academics by school grade may not hone skills of self-tutelage. What is not in question is the observation that children can learn a lot of knowledge in settings other than schools, and in the past most particularly from books. In today's fast-changing world these are important considerations. But there is no question today about the spectacular new availability of knowledge that echoes the glow of the golden swamp of old Amsterdam and now radiates around the world. The swamp in which we find ourselves is global and the gold bobs freely to be grabbed by anyone who reaches into the Internet.

Today's golden swamp is made possible by the packaging of knowledge into digital containers. These containers began as mainframe computers, and evolved into hard drives, floppy disks, CD-roms, and Web pages. The advent of Web pages constituted a major innovation because the container as well as the medium was now radically new. Just like a thought in your head, a Web page has no physical existence; a Web page is no more than a sequencing of zeroes and ones that can inhabit limitless digital storage locations. The medium in which it travels is no more than designations of numbers that make connections among computers that communicate over wires, glass, and radiant waves. Since Web pages have no physical form, I have borrowed one from a verbal illustration by Professor James M. Tour, a chemistry professor at Rice University who is working on harnessing molecules as digital switches. Professor Tour said that when they get single-molecule switches working, "all of human culture in all of human history could fit into something the size of a Coke can."[17] Today, of course, all that knowledge that Professor Tour mentions requires zillions of switches housed on silicon chips. The can-size knowledge treasures in the metaphor for today's knowledge distribution are Web sites containing hunks of things to learn bobbing in the golden swamp of the early 21st century.

The packaging and distribution of knowledge has a history that can be compared to the change in figure 4.3 from the water pump from which a crow is harassing the little girl to the Coke can. The little girl shown hoping to draw water on a farm in 19th century America, and most of her contemporaries, including Abraham Lincoln, drank mainly from the local resources—of water and of knowledge—but distribution and variety improved rapidly in the latter part of that century. In 1886, Atlanta pharmacist John Pemberton was combining some experimental medicinal ingredients and came up with a mixture (secret to this day) that was a caramel-colored liquid with a pleasing fragrance. He took a sample of it down the block to Jacob's Pharmacy where he stirred it into some carbonated water and passed around samples to the drugstore's customers. They liked it and the pharmacy soon began selling it by the glass. Before long the syrup was distributed to other towns and states and people could order Coca-Cola as a soda drink prepared at neighborhood drugstores. Soda fountains have almost

Figure 4.3.   A comparison of access to drinks in the 19th and 20th centuries.

completely disappeared, but back when the inkpots still sat in wells on the desks in my grade school, the soda fountain was important in my daily life. On the walk home after school, I would stop at Fancher's Drug Store and order a "Nightmare." The formula was potent: carbonated water with a squirt of syrup from every single flavor spout. A "fountain Coke," made with a squirt of secret-formula syrup freshly mixed with carbonated water just before you drank it was considered in those days to be superior in taste to bottled Cokes.

Bottling by distributors had been around for half a century by the time I was sipping Nightmares at Fancher's. In 1899, two Chattanooga lawyers, Benjamin F. Thomas and Joseph B. Whitehead, had purchased for one dollar an exclusive license to bottle the beverage from the Coke headquarters in Atlanta where the idea of bottles was looked down on. The company was headed by Asa Candler, who had led it to national prominence. But he missed the future. As Coca-Cola says on its Web site: "Despite being a brilliant and innovative businessman, he didn't realize then that the heart of Coca-Cola would be with a portable bottle beverage customers could take anywhere."[18] In 1964 the first lift-top cans of Coke became available, increasing the portability even more. For a century, since the first bottles were capped in Chattanooga, Tennessee, Coca-Cola has spread its distribution across the United States and the planet with operations in nearly 200 countries by the beginning of the 21st century.

There has been a parallel process in the availability of knowledge. In the figure with the girl and the pump, the knowledge available in her life setting was much like her water supply: she could consume what could be obtained locally. There was, however, an effort in 19th-century America to distribute learning more broadly to children. Horace Mann and Mary Lyon were effective pioneers in taking knowledge to more types of students. Putting it into multiple containers was another major part of the story. William Holmes McGuffey made a contribution that is very likely to have been a part of the experience of the little girl by the pump. His McGuffey Eclectic Readers went through six editions and were widely distributed to 19th-century schools, selling eventually an estimated 122 million copies. They continue in use, republished most recently in 1997. Like Coca-Cola and the soft-drink bottling business in general, textbook publication and educational materials distribution became a major industry during the 20th century. Along with the distribution of textbooks, the "bottling" of specific hunks of knowledge into curricula and the broad distribution of standardized curriculum materials became the mainstream method of modern education.

The two endeavors of bottling and distributing soft drinks and knowledge absolutely lost any similarity when the Internet became the primary location of knowledge. Nothing much has changed for the bottling and distribution of soft drinks since soda fountains passed from the scene and cans augmented bottles. But for the packagers and distributors of knowledge, everything is suddenly different and they may well go the way of the soda fountain. The realization of the new heart of learning is the kind of dramatic turn missed by Asa Candler and the grasp of it has been slow in coming for many in the education establishment. This is the total and spectacular turnaround for knowledge: All students on the planet can now use the same knowledge source—effectively all drink from just one can. That is singularity of scale.

Now it just takes one can! Think about that. Go grab a soft drink and sip it while that sinks in: Everyone will drink from a single can of knowledge without depleting it. Again, the Rosetta Stone Web pages at the British Museum are an example. There is no theoretical limit to the number of learners who could visit those Web pages and absorb the knowledge there into their own minds. They can all do it at the same time. If something is corrected or added, the next time a student imbibes from the Rosetta Stone pages the information will be updated and fresh. The same principle is at work in a system established by the Portland, Oregon, police in which an officer in a squad car can use her wireless device to check mug shots in the department's central database, comparing the remote image of a face with a suspicious individual seen on the street.

Figure 4.4 of a lift-top golden can with the word *knowledge* down the front is a metaphoric image of one or a group of Web pages that contain a particular nugget of knowledge. The example we have used of such a golden can is the Rosetta Stone Web pages on the British Museum Web site. Although it can be found bobbing in the same Internet swamp, the collection of mug shots in the database at the Portland police department does not count as such a can in our discussion. As the portion across the bottom of figure 1.1 depicts, the cans of knowledge are not the only contents of the swamp. Other sorts of things inhabiting the Internet swamp have to do with commerce, personal stuff, pornography, and just about everything else in human affairs. The challenge to learning and education presented now by the Internet swamp, made golden by the cans bobbing within it, is to locate and drink from the cans of knowledge that represent what John Dewey called organizing bodies of truth we call studies.

Figure 4.4. A figurative nugget of knowledge.

Who cannot envy those drugstore shoppers at Jacob's who happened to be there the day the first Coke was tasted? The crew who sailed the Half Moon up and down the Hudson gained bragging rights for having seen a great river first for Europe. It is a privilege and joy to be present at the creation. In that vein, I am amazed by and grateful for the very good luck to have watched some of the first golden cans of knowledge plunging into the Internet swamp, and to spend the next four years observing and working with the phenomenon as it has transferred the primary locus of human knowledge to a new location. I believe it is the most profound change for the handling of human knowledge since the invention of writing, and perhaps more important even than that. We called the project I headed during the goldening of the Internet swamp HomeworkHeaven.com (still my favorite name for it), and then NoSweat.com (because it was so easy to find what you needed to study), and finally HomeworkCentral.com (the name it retains at bigchalk.com where it is now located). By the time I left the project in May 2001, we had assembled about 150,000 links to golden cans and linked them into about 35,000 study topics. Although I chose the links we used during the first few months at the close of 1997, the cascade of academic pages flowing onto the Internet, and the increasing depth and breadth of the knowledge they carried, soon moved beyond my generalist knowledge. We hired graduate students to expand my team in 1998 and in 2000 put a Ph.D. in charge of humanities and another one in charge of the sciences.

When I began looking for nuggets of knowledge on the Internet it was May 1997. Surfing was still great fun and its results were essentially successful and comprehensive when I was looking for something specific. Some major digital projects were already online, such as the one named for Gutenberg that digitized text and that had been under way before the World Wide Web caused the Internet explosion. Important institutions like the Library of Congress and NASA were placing assets online in a major way. Imaginative college instructors were putting up Web pages to complement their hard-copy syllabi. The venerable World Lecture Hall began growing in 1994 on the University of Texas Web site under the visionary guidance of UT's first webmaster, Richard Mendez.[19] I remember my excitement when I first found the collection at the World Lecture Hall because I could go through the online postings from college instructors from many schools to link to nuggets of knowledge that they had included among class schedules and other administrative material. The World Lecture Hall remains an excellent site to visit to find those sorts of nuggets today, as well as to browse through to get a sense of how Web pages have been developed by instructors at colleges and universities. For the first couple of years I worked on our project it seemed like everybody who knew something was putting it into a virtual can and tossing it into the Internet. Some things were particularly popular because they were obviously better and more compelling on a Web page than they were in print. Periodic tables of elements and calculators to convert everything imaginable showed up—several at first and then dozens. A few hundred quality links for the study disciplines—golden cans of knowledge, to use our metaphor—in the mid-1990s became a few thousand, and many thousands by the end of the decade.

It was the most fascinating thing I had ever watched, and I began to notice some controlling factors. For one thing, there was not a need for 10 or 20 or 100 periodic tables of elements online. It makes more sense for everyone to use the best table. But who is to judge among them? The Google search site appeared and was an instant hit because it put the links the most people went to at the top of its list of sites found in a search. That should mean that gradually the best periodic table of elements would rise to the top of the list because it would have been chosen by the experience of its users. That was an excellent way to make the choice—a pragmatic exercise of peer review. Other factors began to operate to give links prominence. In the example of the Rosetta Stone pages, the prestige of their hosting British Museum and the fact that the actual stone is housed by the museum are good reasons to learn what the pages offer. A few other Web pages on the subject of the stone may be called for, to amplify or dissent from the British Museum materials. The Cleveland Museum of Art has some educational kids pages with a cartoon guide named Rosetta Stone,[20] who wears a pith helmet and introduces children to mummies and pharaohs. In the example of the Rosetta Stone, about six Web sites with knowledge nuggets should suffice; a sample group can be viewed at EdClicks.com. This six-pack of golden cans could quench the world's thirst and allow anyone and everyone to become knowledgeable about the Rosetta Stone. The single six-pack takes the place of the page in a school textbook printed in a quantity of many thousands and of pages in books in hundreds of libraries. Moving into the future, there will be little if any theoretical reason to have partial references to the Rosetta Stone printed on thousands, or millions, of scattered pages, which are of course not interactive nor linked to unlimited related information and context.

We are now well into the trend where much of the new knowledge being developed will never find its way onto paper. In 1997 the Theban Mapping Project[21] Web site began digitally chronicling the excavations in the ancient Egyptian Valley of the Kings. Printed publication of materials from this sort of Web site occurs secondarily, if at all. All of what is being learned at Thebes is available online soon after it is discovered and thereafter all the time to anyone on the planet through the project's Web site. A high percentage of knowledge growing today out of scientific research goes first to the Internet and often never to print. Images from the Hubble Telescope, for example, abound on the Internet and can be checked out at EdClicks.com in the *Watch Knowledge Grow* section where it is posted with other Web pages containing things to learn that are continually updated. The U.S. Printing Office continues to print Capitol Hill's venerable Congressional Directory on paper, but beginning in 1999 it offered continuous online revisions, explaining: "No printed counterpart will exist for these online publication revisions but when a new printed publication is required, the process will be greatly simplified due to the existence of the updated versions."[22] All the virtual containers of knowledge mentioned in this paragraph are created and maintained as an original source and do not require replication based on the number of users. Users may scale (increase in number) yet their quantity related to a knowledge page remains singular: one Web page serves a single user or billions of users. Knowledge itself has no scale at all. Algebra is algebra; there is no way to multiply algebra and no longer any need to run off thousands of copies of its theorems. Now called Math2.org, the mathematics Web site that Dave Manura has maintained online since 1995 has made math tables and fundamentals available to millions upon millions of users who include school students, teachers, and the public.

After the first flood of knowledge had surged into the Internet, the natural trend for users to go to the best offerings for each topic began to stem the tide. A winnowing process set in that began to cut back the number of cans for a given topic because everyone would drink from the best can for every knowledge nugget. As I watched the knowledge gold within the swamp began to be refined by those inherent processes, an even more potent limitation to its ultimate growth became clear: while the number of users could grow to billions, the amount of knowledge would grow very little, just at its edges. We can expect a new generation of millions of kids every few years who need to learn algebra, but we cannot realistically expect very much more algebra, if any at all. There will be no more Roman history except from a rare new fragment discovered now and then. We probably will find no more sayings of Confucius or plays by Shakespeare. French grammar will not change much. There will be more astronomy and biotechnology, but fundamentals of these and other sciences will seldom change. More will be learned about the pharaohs of Thebes, but most of what is already known will not change. As I mentioned, in the project that became HomeworkCentral.com, we developed 35,000 study topics. They include the big ones like math and the little ones within those, like equilateral triangles. They include repetitive topics, like the history of every country, that add up quickly to make many dozens of topics. Although many more topics could be added to the 35,000, they would be more and more detailed and of interest to fewer and fewer students. The standard bigger topics are all there already and even the diminishing level of detail finds its limit. For example, the history topics descend to detail from the history of: Texas to San Antonio to The Alamo to Davy Crockett; and Davy is a topic that will show up as well in other topics: Tennessee, Congress, and Beaver Hats. This efficiency is almost dumbfounding: all the world can drink from the single can of Davy's biography. No need to mix up other batches, or bottle and ship anything. The knowledge just sits there in ones and zeroes ready to show up on any device that interfaces the Internet.

It turns out that our current challenge is not repetitively bottling and distributing knowledge nuggets, but finding the best ones in the swamp. Today we are faced with an Internet into which our knowledge resources have been tossed like beverage cans into a lake that has become swamped by all sorts of growth and trash. A scientist puts a Web page online with an instructive animation that would be helpful to students in her field. It joins millions upon millions of other pages in the swamp. The two broad methods that have been used over the early years of the Internet for finding a useful Web page are hearsay and word searches. The hearsay method works quite well within discrete knowledge topics but word searches are foundering in the enormous and expanding Internet. I would be happy to see word searches pass from the scene because they are flawed in at least three fundamental ways. First, they depend on a process at least one step removed from human assessment of what they land on: the meaning assigned to the word they find. That meaning can be right, but it is not always right. A lot of brilliant work has been done to improve searching and perhaps one day it will be able to interpret content meaning as well as people can. That will not overcome the second, far worse problem: search engines miss the newest and freshest materials on the Internet and cannot find pages that are generated dynamically because those pages do not exist until they are requested. Third—and this is cognitive chaos—the search engines are clueless about the context of the links they return. The best results I can get from searching for "Rosetta Stone" is a fairly even mix of links to Web sites about the Egyptian antiquity, some software named "Rosetta Stone," and a rock band by the same name. The dexterous talent of digital combining to bring along context will be discussed soon. Search engines do not achieve this effect; they do the opposite. Students who do text-search research on the Internet already need to know a lot about what they are looking for to come up with words that will bring up useful links; they also must expect the links to arrive with no relationship among themselves except that they all contain the same string of letters.

Fairly early in my experience, metasites began to appear online where webmasters endeavored to list all the links on the Internet for a particular subject. The subjects tended to be very big ones: chemistry, engineering, and the like. Although the metasites were and are good places to browse for entry points into what I call hearsay miniwebs, they are not as helpful as the miniwebs. The metasites end up being lists of links that are not related into context. They tend to be alphabetical lists by title instead of contextual links by granular subject. Related links by hearsay are better because they do a good job of locating and organizing some knowledge on the Internet. This process has gone on from the earliest days of the cyber medium; it is a natural outgrowth of the essential bottom-up character of the Internet. The word *hearsay* implies a process that is loose and unconfirmed. It means rumor or basing what you recommend on someone else's opinion. Those definitions are a pretty accurate description of the typical "related links" listing that very often appear on Web sites that cover academic subjects. In the picture of the swamp in figure 1.1, the golden cans are linked by some lines from one to another. Using Internet parlance and our metaphor: the webmaster for one of the cans points to other cans he or she recommends for related knowledge. In my own experience of building collections of links for specific topics, I have found that moving along the hearsay pointers from one site to the next is the best way to find quality links and to approach being comprehensive for what is available on the Internet for the topic I am researching. The more specific the topic, the more effective the hearsay approach: the expert who has made a Web page on his expertise will have heard about other Web offerings for his topic and will say what they are on his own page. He is an ideal expert to evaluate the quality of outside links and to choose the ones worth listing. He virtually hears about other good links, opens them up and evaluates them, and if he approves of their content he says to go and try them. Other Web hosts in his field are doing the same for their pages, and the miniweb is formed and grows. When you find yourself moving within some hearsay connections you will be able to explore a topic from Web site to Web site following the suggestions of the experts in the topic you are studying.

I have illustrated the flow of knowledge onto the Internet as an outpouring of gold from throughout the world into the swamp that is the Internet. The remainder of the book contains my thoughts on what can be done to use the new location and manifestations of what is known by humankind in the future. There are two aspects to the work I have described in the pages that follow. The first has to do with the nuggets of knowledge: how to use new and old arts, skills, and intellectual methods to interface topics maximizing the cognitive powers of the digital medium. The second is about showcasing the digital knowledge assets in context through a virtual world's fair everyone on Earth can attend.

What will become of the swamp? My suggestion is that we ignore it. Trying to straighten it out and worrying about putting everything into a proper place is neither productive nor possible. Such attempts are like trying to organize the grains of sand in the Sahara Desert. It is equal folly, I think, to try to find a Web page by searching every word—again, that is like looking at every grain of the Sahara's sand when you need to find just one. The Internet will remain a swamp in terms of the overall meaning of what it contains and it will resist any attempt to organize it from the top down. The Internet is a communications hook-up, not a book or library. Within it have grown myriad excellent new Weblets, like the one the Portland police use to connect officers to their database of mug shots. Already within the swamp are many Weblets on study subjects. I have listed samples of them at EdClicks.com on the Study Subject Weblets section. Clicking through the links listed there will introduce you to the hearsay routing through topics. In my visual metaphor, the Weblets are the cans of knowledge linked within the swamp.

The Internet is a golden swamp. It is a limitless environment in which it is possible to construct entities of meaning from the bottom up by combining the smallest grains into gobs, and the gobs into gestalts, which have greater meaning than the sums of their parts. Related gestalts gather into context. It is wonderful and beautiful. Let's move ahead by exploring how a digital can of knowledge, which is a very simple model for a container of knowledge, can be morphed into an expressive new entity—like Dopey.

NOTES

1. Bryony Coles and John Coles, *People of the Wetlands: Bogs, Bodies and Lake-Dwellers* (New York: Thames and Hudson, 1989), 76.

2. Coles and Coles, 32.

3. Coles and Coles, 32.

4. Paul Zumthor, *Daily Life in Rembrandt's Holland* (Stanford, Calif.: Stanford University Press, 1994), 10.

5. The Pilgrim Hall Museum, www.pilgrimhall.org/bradfordjournalleiden.htm [accessed 2 August 2001].

6. Christopher Brown, Jan Kelch, and Pieter van Thiel, *Rembrandt: The Master & His Workshop, Paintings* (New Haven, Conn.: Yale University Press, 1991), 42.

7. University of California at Berkeley Web site, www.ucmp.berkeley.edu/history/leeuwenhoek.html [accessed 2 August 2001].

8. Brown, Kelch, and van Thiel, *Rembrandt,* 53.

9. Anthony Bailey, *Rembrandt's House* (Boston: Houghton Mifflin, 1978), 30.

10. John Dewey, "The Child and the Curriculum," in *Dewey on Education,* ed. Martin S. Dworkin (New York: Teachers College Press, 1959), 97.

11. Jon Wiles, *Curriculum Essentials: A Resource of Educators* (Boston: Allyn and Bacon, 1999), 5–6.

12. Zumthor, *Rembrandt's Holland,* 99–100.

13. Zumthor, *Rembrandt's Holland,* 103.

14. Zumthor, *Rembrandt's Holland,* 103.

15. Zumthor, *Rembrandt's Holland,* 219.

16. Zumthor, *Rembrandt's Holland,* 220.

17. Kenneth Chang, "Clever Wiring Harnesses Tiny Switches," *New York Times on the Web: Science Times,* 17 July 2001, www.nytimes.com/2001/07/17/science/physical/17SWIT.html [accessed 17 July 2001].

18. *Coca-Cola,* "Company Overview," www2.Coca-Cola.com/about/index.html [accessed 5 October 2001].

19. *World Lecture Hall,* wnt.cc.utexas.edu/~wlh/about/history.cfm [accessed 9 October 2001].

20. *Cleveland Museum of Art,* "Fun for Kids Online," www.clemusart.com/archive/pharaoh/rosetta/ [accessed 9 October 2001].

21. *Theban Mapping Project,* www.kv5.com/intro.html [accessed 30 September 2001].

22. U.S. Congress, *Congressional Directory,* www.access.gpo.gov/congress/cong016.html [accessed 10 September 2001].

5

HOW THE ARTISTS WILL CONTRIBUTE

What Is Dopey?

The first time the world saw Disney dwarf Dopey, he was inside a mine sweeping rejected diamonds into a dustpan. He walked over to a table where the senior dwarf, Doc, was sorting stones, picked up two of the fat gems, placed them in his eyes, grinned at Doc and swung full-face into the camera. Soon the seven dwarfs quit their day's work in the mine and Dopey is seen swinging a big bag toward the storage room a couple of times and then flying with the bag that he had not let go of, through the door into the dark. He comes out, locks the door with a key, almost forgets to hang the key on a peg on the door jam, and then joins the other dwarfs on their march home. As they go single file through the woods singing "Hi ho, hi ho, home from work we go," Dopey is last in line and never does get into step. In the fall of 2001 Dopey once more trotted out his stuff, this time in the edgiest digital realm, as the movie in which he starred 64 years earlier was released with a major advertising blast on DVD.

The credits at the beginning of the classic *Snow White and the Seven Dwarfs*, where we first meet Dopey and which is the first full-length animated movie feature, state that the story is adapted from the Grimms' Fairy Tales. In the original story by the brothers who wrote the classic tale, the seven dwarfs searched the mountains for copper and gold ore. Though warm and caring, the personality of the dwarfs was collective with no individuals named. There is no hint of a Dopey in the Grimms' tale. Although the plot is generally the same in the original story as the movie, there are significant differences that maximize the expressive pallet of motion in the film, and other parts from the original Grimms that the adapters must have decided would not work well on screen are skipped in the Disney version. For example, when Snow White finds the home of the little dwarfs in the original, it is immaculately clean. What would the movie be without the animals helping Snow White surprise the dwarfs by cleaning their messy house, or minus touches like Grumpy complaining because his cup has been washed and its sugar ring is gone? There are no forest animals in the Grimms' original, and the animals are one of the most lively and entertaining aspects of the film. Dopey was not even in the original script for the Disney version, and like other characters who are among Disney's most winsome, Jiminy Cricket and the rabbit Thumper, Dopey joined the cast after the animation was under way in the story where he eventually starred.[1] What is Dopey? Among many interesting and charming things, he is a superb example of something made possible by the advent of a new medium. We will take a look at Dopey and how he came about, to see what he might be able to tell us about how we could do exciting new things with the digital and Internet media.

Paul T. Burns' handsome Web site, *The Complete History of the Discovery of Cinematography*,[2] relates how the technical world was developed that eventually constructed the nursery where Dopey was born. Burns presents the motion picture habitat where Dopey lives as a progression of technical achievements over a period of 2,500 years. His chronology ends with the close of the 19th century, when the essential technology for movies was in place. Dopey's entrance into our hearts and culture was dependent on innovators who developed photography and set it in motion, following one after another through the centuries. Archimedes and Da Vinci contributed, as did Dutchman Christiaan Huygens. Nineteenth century tech guys included Daguerre, Eastman, and Edison.

Dopey is also the product of cartoon animation, which stands on a specialized technical platform. One of the first artists to appreciate the possibilities of cinematography for cartoons was Frenchman Emile Cohl (1857–1938). The root of the word *cinema* is the Greek word *kinemat,* meaning "motion." Cohl, who drew strip cartoons for print media, was aware that apparent motion could be achieved by going quickly from drawing to drawing, frame by frame. This was quite a change from the static drawings of the time like the one in figure 5.1, where the artist crammed all the action into a single drawing. Cohl and countryman George Melies made the technical advance of putting sequential drawings on film from which they could be projected on a screen, and in 1908 created a film cartoon series based on a little man called Fantoche. Theirs were some of the first stop-frame films, and using film in this way was a key technical step toward the possibility of Dopey. As a matter of fact, essentially every technical step it would take to create Dopey had been accomplished. There was no technical reason in 1908 why a studio could not have produced characters just as enchanting, entertaining, and expressive as those in the great pivotal cartoon features produced by Walt Disney in the latter half of the 1930s. It is almost as true that no character any more expressively complex or engaging than those who debuted in the 1930s has since been added to the cartoon pantheon.

The world of Web sites entered the 21st century in a very similar state of maturation as that in which cinematography found itself as it began the 20th century: the technology is in place but the expressiveness of content is, to be generous, undeveloped. Of course, technology continued to contribute throughout

Figure 5.1. This drawing of dwarfs playing baseball is from a 19th-century card promoting Sweet Home family soap.

the 20th century to the motion picture industry, supporting and enhancing it in many ways, including the major additions of sound and color and, most recently, digital effects. A different sort of progress was also accomplished in repositioning the performing arts from theaters to sequential photographs on projected film, and then in developing new genres of performing arts that took advantage of new possibilities inherent in the film medium. One wonderfully exploited possibility was the ability of cameras to capture new visual experiences that were fascinating and stunning, including great scenic beauty, intimate portrayals of nature, and magnified views of the microscopic world. Old forms of art and entertainment were repositioned. New ones were invented. The Web site industry's future will be transformed by these same processes, and that is a very good thing.

The animated cartoon is a wonderfully pure example of a tech-supported cinematic innovation that took on a life of its own. Although others made significant contributions, it is not a serious overstatement to say that the animated cartoon was elevated to an art in the Disney studios in the mid-1930s. Led by Walt and his famed Nine Old Men, the animators at Disney progressed in their creative achievements that are obvious in the comparison of a 1932 Disney short cartoon film called *Babes in the Woods* and the 1937 feature-length *Snow White.* In the 1932 production, a crowd of little men, looking much like the baseball dwarfs in figure 5.1, are made to move. The little men appear to have been stamped by the same cookie cutter. Like the dwarfs in the Grimms' version of *Snow White,* the personality of the seven is collective: they look alike, move in a group, and have similar facial expressions. In 1937 the seven dwarfs each have a name to match their seven distinct and entertaining personalities. Whatever else Dopey may be, he was no accident. The effort and talent that went into creating the expression of personalities in pioneering cartoon films at Disney was intense and enormous.

A generation before the Disney animators established the personalities of its characters, Winsor McCay created Gertie the Dinosaur, whose expressiveness earned McCay the title of the father of the animated cartoon. Gertie was entirely the vision and product of McCay, who drew her and produced her in short cartoons from 1911 to 1921. Gertie's elaborate birthing, that lasted months for a single five-minute cartoon, was expensive. Soon the more cost-effective studio method for making movie cartoons was developed, where specialists handled particular phases of the production, and McCay groaned, "Animation should be an art. . . . What you fellows have done with it is making it into a trade . . . not an art, but a trade . . . bad luck."[3] It is an oversimplification but essentially true that for the first three decades of the 20th century the animated cartoons that were produced were little more than repositioned drawings of gags set in motion on screens by the exciting new technology of cinema—motion pictures.

The infant Internet has also been bereft of artistic emphasis or achievement. In the first place, early on just getting text sent and displayed challenged the most stalwart patience. Images, or even type fonts, required too much file space, clogging the circuits and overflowing server storage capacity. Even so, artists have looked to a better day. In 1996, David Siegel wrote a popular book called *Creating Killer Web Sites*.[4] He concluded his introduction to the book with these words:

> The Web is here to stay. I hope this book helps designers to make the transition. In her essay titled "Electronic Typography," Jessica Helfand, a brilliant designer who has turned her modem into a design tool, wrote: "Here is the biggest contribution to communication technology to come out of the last decade, a global network linking some 50 million people worldwide, and designers—communication designers, no less—are nowhere to be found." With the freedom of the Web comes new responsibility; it will take new thinking to make the Web more visually rewarding as it continues to grow more interesting.

Four years later, highly respected Web guru Jakob Nielsen's book *Designing Web Usability* became a popular primer for the Internet industry. Nielsen begins the book by stating flatly: "Usability rules the Web. Simply stated, if the customer can't find a product then he or she will not buy it."[5] He began his chapter titled "Content Design" with this analogy:

> Ultimately, users visit your Web site for its content. Everything else is just the backdrop. The design is there to allow people access to the content. The old analogy is somebody who goes to see a theater performance: When they leave the theater, you want them to be discussing how great the *play* was and not how great the costumes were. [emphasis Nielson's][6]

There is a tendency these days in Internet circles to see navigation and usability as separate from content. Perhaps they are separated now, but in a better visual and interactive world everything is seamless communication. What is Dopey and how does he relate to his costume? Is he a technical achievement? Is he design? Is he content? Why is there more to him than what is found in a little man from figure 5.1? My answer is that he is made up of parts that are technical, design, and content—however, Dopey is actually more than the sum of his parts. To experience and enjoy Dopey on screen is to comprehend meaning that would not exist in focusing on the technique that projects him, or the colors that play off of his figure, or the looseness of his clothes. I realize Jakob Nielson is making the same point when he says you should not remember just the costumes, and I agree. The key, I believe, comes from Walt Disney: you approach creating communication through artistic method and vision. When this is done well, I believe the perplexity over usability and navigation on the Internet will disappear. I believe this is infinitely more true and important for knowledge nuggets than it is for more commercial subjects, like listing stock prices. Still, for any subject, using visual ideas is very powerful if done well. If we continue to dissect communication into issues of usability and navigation, we will make no significant elevation of communication on the Internet. Dopey is manifested by a synergy. Until we are able to achieve this same expressive synergy with Web sites we remain in the infancy of our medium. Fiefdoms of technology people, design people, content people, usability people, business people, and education people can only bog down progress. That is no different than what was going on in the animation of movies in the first decades of the 20th century. As Winsor McCay said, bad luck.

Looking at the ingredients that combined to produce true innovation in animated features commencing with Snow White and her seven dwarf friends in the late 1930s provides some enlightening comparisons to the current infancy of Internet interfaces. For animated cartoons, the tech people ruled as the 19th century closed, earning "oohs" and "ahs" from motion attained by flipping and then flashing simple and awkward stick-figure drawings in front of excited viewers. The visionary McCay showed before 1920 that his Gertie could have expressive personality. But in his time, the business "suits" looked at the bottom line and the assembly line studio method raised efficiency above the quest for expressiveness.

The achievements of the Disney studio in the 1930s that made Dopey possible, and then a reality, were guided by art. Walt Disney began as an artist himself, assembled artists as the primary studio team and hired other artists to teach them all so they could attain higher artistic levels in their output. The challenge they all tackled was harnessing the new technology that would project frame after frame, creating the illusion of movement. That was not easy and they were plow-ing new ground. Bringing to mind for me of some of the debacles I have seen and participated in while trying to make some pages work in a Web site, this is an ac-count from the early days at Disney:

> The old man had little personality, but he had to be old and kindly. . . . The ani-mator was determined to get a shuffling walk, a bent posture, and a feeling of age in the movements. He did not want this man to reach far, take big steps, or in any way appear athletic or strong. The layout man had drawn a door on a wall that had a true storybook feeling about it, but, unfortunately, the doorknob was on the far side of the door, a long distance from the elderly shopkeeper. He had to walk over close enough to reach out easily and grasp it. But this left him standing directly in the path of the door, which for some reason opened inward!
>
> Two years after this, the animator would have run back to the Music Room and screamed about restricting the layout. . . . But this option had not been considered at the time. . . . That animator, with great determination, attacked the problem from an action standpoint, probably hoping secretly that he would show everyone how well he could analyze the situation. The door opened four inches and hit the gentleman's foot. He stepped back in a casual, shuffling manner. He opened the door another four inches only to find that he had bumped against his other foot. Again he stepped back—another four inches. Now the door was against the first foot once more. There was no way he could step back far enough into the scene to clear this door, and the farther he backed up the more problem there would be in walking around the obstruction to get outside, where he had to be by the end of the scene. So as the film rolled by, the poor man shuffled around endlessly as the door gradually opened enough for him to reverse his steps and struggle into the night. It was a comedy of errors on everyone's part, but the animator bore the brunt of the kidding more than the director or the layout man. There was much to be learned.[7]

None of the animator's problems with this old man had anything to do with technology. Other lessons had to be learned before the studio could give birth to Dopey. In a similar way, Web sites as we now know them present us with a gamut of nontechnical problems that tend to be lumped together under the trendy title of usability, which joins its cousin navigation as the ugly ducklings of the Inter-net. Like the tests for school kids that are trendy too, what makes these ducklings ugly is that the expectations for them are too low. Is it really a major victory just to find a Web page? That should be a given. Jef Raskin says we are oppressed by our electronic servants.[8] He says, "I reject the idea that computers are difficult to use because what we do with them has become irretrievably complicated. No matter how complex the task a product is trying to accomplish, the simple parts of the task should remain simple."[9] The task did not get simpler for the animator trying to get the old man through the door because the door was incorrectly designed to allow the character of the man to be expressed. If the animator had wanted to establish an athletic young guy the door would have been perfect. In one leap and grab the younger character could have bounced through the door and expressed his essence. These are artistic considerations.

Walt Disney stepped back from domination by technology and came at animation through art. In my view, the web's ducklings of usability and navigation are still ugly because they are still creatures of technology and are not yet understood as creatures of expression. When they are they will become graceful swans. Cumbersome as they are today, they cannot now be Dopey. There is much to be learned. Many of the lessons are the same as those learned at Disney. Two of the Nine Old Men, Frank Thomas and Ollie Johnston, explained that creating a visual language was a primary factor. They quote another member of their team, John Hench, who said, "We learned here about using images to communicate—to develop a kind of visual literacy."[10] There are important efforts under way to standardize visual language on the Internet, where conventions such as underlining text to indicate it is clickable are well-established. This is laudable, and it is my hope that in the future the standards are advanced by artists instead of the techies for whom the fact that underlining impairs legibility would not be on their radar screen. In an even better world, the tech guy defers to artists when artistic judgments are to be made. There should not be a conflict between tech and art, but we need to remember that tech makes the button clickable but it is art that ascribes meaning to the experience triggered by the click. In discussing the visual language authored at Disney, Thomas and Johnston quote violinist Isaac Stern, who when asked what distinguished a truly great artist responded: "The ability to communicate." Thomas and Johnston conclude about communication and their boss: "[Communication] is the key ingredient in every art form and certainly the great strength of Walt Disney's genius."[11] Communication is also the goal of Web pages.

Walt Disney did not ignore technology. He encouraged and embraced it, ever willing to employ technical innovations to advance the animation art. But he approached them from the direction of his primary artistic craft. The distinction between the roles of tech and art in animation is evident in the career of Earl Hurd, who managed to make contributions to both. In 1914 he patented the use of transparent celluloid in the assembling of cartoon frames. The important technical invention, quickly adopted by all animators, allowed them to draw static backgrounds only once and then to draw the characters' moves on sequential transparent cels, as they were quickly nicknamed. Two decades later Hurd joined the Disney staff as an artist and won Walt's admiration for a series of clever, expressive ideas. Hurd was placed in the Disney Story Department and contributed several gags to Snow White, like the one where Dopey gets sneezed out of his long coat. Hurd's contribution to animation of the cel was a technical one; his gags that were added to productions were artistic. Getting sneezed out of your coat communicates—expresses—your personality. The cel was important because it saved having to make a lot of duplicate drawings and added to the bottom line; but the cel is not expressive. It is a technical platform to be appreciated but not looked to for clues of expression.

The Internet is a means of communication that so far has been mostly carried out through text because transmissions of more exciting materials are still slow and artistic designers have thus far played a minor role. However, the Internet is already being lifted toward its expressive potential. We have quite a few Gerties to prove expression is possible. Gertie's creator blamed the business suits for restricting the bottom line. I think the problem with Web expressiveness is different, caused by download delays in the first years of the Internet and on sidetracking into isolating usability as something considered separate from expression. Before leaving Gertie, though, it is worth pointing out that the bottom-line restrictions that demanded the studio production method and stunted the development of the animated cartoon were not what created the multimillion-dollar animated cartoon industry. What did that was the artistic and initially very expensive expressiveness invented and mastered at Disney. A broad pallet of the expressive animation ideas won by the huge investment and hard work at Disney remains in use today, still serving in large part to paint the joy and fun of cartoon animation and making that now senior citizen of cinema Dopey, born in 1937, a 2001 DVD star even while he collects his Social Security and the potential injuries from his frequent falls are covered by Medicare.

The time is now for inventing new artistic forms for Web site interface expressiveness: the measure of art is communication, as Isaac Stern put it. The converse is equally true: communication, though it rests upon technical platforms, is measured by art. At the expressive level art and communication are the same thing, but we do not need to plum the aesthetics here. It is very important practically, however, to realize that the Internet and the digital medium it conveys form a fabulous new tool for the communication of ideas through new means and forms of expression. There lies as yet enormous untapped potential for establishing wonderful new cyber sources for interfacing the study disciplines. The time has passed for just putting a topic in a can and tossing it into the swamp. The challenge becomes how to express concepts and facts to be learned, like fractions and fractals, Canada and chemistry, French and frogs, mummies and the Mississippi. The Internet sites listed on EdClicks.com for the subjects just mentioned are examples of how these topics are already expressed on outstanding Web creations. But I do not think our digital and Internet industry has as yet been elevated by an intensive focus on forming digital tools of expression in a manner similar to the elevation of animation from static gags to artistic expression achieved by the Disney team in the 1930s. The few expressively excellent Web pages that float in the swamp are rare creatures, like Gertie the Dinosaur was in the jerky, stilted, stick-figure world of early 20th-century cartoon animation. How to increase expressive quality and comprehensiveness for all studies, and how to make them globally accessible, are subjects of this book.

Here are some definitions of *expression* from Webster's Dictionary:[12] "An act, process, or instance of representing in a medium (as words) . . . something that manifests, embodies, or symbolizes something else . . . a mode, means, or use of significant representation or symbolism." An empty Web page, like a blank cel, represents nothing until it displays something. (For the nitpickers, of course, one of them does represent the essence of a Web page and the other the essence of a cel, but that is not relevant here. What counts is the meaning of what is displayed on the visual ground offered by the technology.) In the case of either blank visual surface, once the *tabula rasa* has been marked, something is going to be expressed. Smearing on marks and colors with his little fingers may (though we don't know) represent objects or ideas to an infant as he admires his work, but to a casual observer what is expressed is confusion or chaos. Once the smearing has been done, the patterns created defy, or at least severely limit, cognitive enhancement. I think the same problem exists with the legion of Web sites into which gobs of words, images, and buttons have been smeared. In the vast majority of cases, improving the communication from such Web sites is, in the best-case scenario, expensive and complex—and more frequently, nearly impossible.

We should look at the next phase of Web development as a thorough start-over for artistry and expression. I think most people experienced in the Web world would agree with what I have been saying. Seldom, if ever, does a webmaster pronounce pride in a finished, perfected site. Far more frequently, the comment goes something like, "We are in the middle of redesign and you're really going to like the new version."

Looking once again at the seven dwarfs from *Snow White*, it seems clear that figures from static drawings like those of the little men playing baseball in figure 5.1 were not revised into Disney's seven dwarfs because there is barely anything in such figures to suggest seven different personalities: Doc, Bashful, Grumpy, Happy, Sleepy, Sneezy, and Dopey. There was nothing, either, in the tale by the Grimm Brothers where the story usually relates that the dwarfs, as a group, did this or that. Even when they act individually, there is very little to suggest individual personalities when the Grimms are telling the story:

> The first said, who has been sitting on my chair. The second, who has been eating off my plate. The third, who has been taking some of my bread. The fourth, who has been eating my vegetables. The fifth, who has been using my fork. The sixth, who has been cutting with my knife. The seventh, who has been drinking out of my mug. Then the first looked round and saw that there was a little hollow on his bed, and he said, who has been getting into my bed. The others came up and each called out, somebody has been lying in my bed too. But the seventh when he looked at his bed saw little snow-white, who was lying asleep therein. And he called the others, who came running up, and they cried out with astonishment, and brought their seven little candles and let the light fall on little snow-white. Oh, heavens, oh, heavens, cried they, what a lovely child. And they were so glad that they did not wake her up, but let her sleep on in the bed. And the seventh dwarf slept with his companions, one hour with each, and so passed the night.[13]

The personalities of the seven dwarfs in the movie were the artistic invention of the animators at the Disney Studios—devised and executed to maximize the expressive potential of the new medium of cartoon animation supported by the technology of cinematography. Walt Disney, and Winsor McCay before him, understood that the medium was new. They saw that a powerful form of entertainment expression might be possible, and they realized that to achieve it new expressive forms and language had to be invented. Gertie the Dinosaur hinted at what could be possible. After several years of intense effort the animators presented Dopey and his ilk to the world. Certainly he was winsome and entertaining, but when Dopey debuted in 1937 most fundamentally, he was new. He could not have entertained us without the technical invention of repeated frames projected from film. Pasting a sequence of the old sort of static cartoon drawings on to the repeated frames had not achieved much expression. The technology had given the artists a strange new kind of stage which existed only in the dimension of time. Writing in 1934, at the time the Disney crew were getting down to serious work, Rudolf Arnheim suggests one of the ways in which the canvas of time was new for artists using pencils and brushes:

> The motion picture specializes in presenting events. It shows changes in time. This preference is explained by the nature of the medium. A motion picture in itself is an event: it looks different every moment, whereas there is no such temporal progress in a painting or sculpture. Motion being one of its outstanding properties, the film is required by aesthetic law to use and interpret motion. . . .
>
> Motion not only serves to inform the audience of the events that make up the story. It is also highly expressive. When we watch a mother putting her child to bed we not only understand what is going on but also learn from the calm or hasty, smooth or fumbling, energetic or weak, sure or hesitant gestures of the mother what kind of person she is, how she feels at the particular moment, and what her relationship is to her child.[14]

Arnheim, as he always does, hits the nail on the head. Film radiates expression by using motion. Two years after Arnheim wrote the paragraphs above, Disney artist Roy Williams spent two days doodling out ideas for a scene for Dopey. John Canemaker describes Williams in creative action, working in the medium of motion:

> "Dopey & the Shoes" is the title [Williams] gave to pages of ideas for a sequence in which the dumbest of the seven dwarfs discovers under his robe an extra pair of shoes that have a life of their own. On a single sheet of paper (dated September 9, 1936), Williams played with stream-of-consciousness sketches of passive Dopey led by the aggressive magical shoes: forced to walk in a circle on all fours, lifted off the ground, hopping ("a la goat," wrote Williams) run backwards, and kicked in the face ("Socko").
>
> On several more pages, Williams attempted to form a continuity of the gags by putting them sequentially into small boxes (as in prestoryboard days). The scene

begins with Dopey's hands becoming wedged in (or captured by) the enchanted shoes, which come to life and hop forward. That led Williams to a new idea: the shoes do a dance "split" and Dopey falls on his nose, and so on through a series of pulls, hits, hops, and crash landings. A page of drawings (dated September 10, 1936) suggests how to "get rid of shoes," or more accurately, how the shoes might get rid of Dopey. They do so by scampering under a chair, where even the smallest dwarf cannot fit.[15]

About 40 years after it became possible to flip a series of drawings in a machine and project them, major achievements were made with tools of the medium to create new forms of expression. Winsor McCay showed some of the potential two decades before things were really cooking at Disney. Expressiveness on the Internet is yet to be invented in any focused or organized manner. Other innovations of the new cyber medium have been exploited very powerfully, including e-mail communication, e-commerce, and the provision of instant access to all kind of information. Huge amounts of text have been made available online, including just about all of the world's major literature, much of which can be downloaded into increasingly attractive e-books. Images abound, from art, astronomy, biology, technology, news, and elsewhere. But thus far we have taken few steps toward achieving a level of creative innovation to anything like Dopey. Creatures of a new form of expressiveness do not yet greet us on our monitors. There are hints, but they tend to drown in everything else that occupies the screen. I am not trying to be critical but provocative, especially concerning learning materials.

Walt Disney and his animators invented a new visual language and expressive art that harnessed the opportunities for drawn images that did not exist before they could be set in motion. As the developers of cinematography gave what became the art of animated cartoons a technical platform, so the Internet has created a new platform to express just about anything, including for our purposes what John Dewey called the organizing bodies of truth that we call studies. Web expression is a new art of the future poised for invention by those who are able to lift their sights above the past and present. Many of the study disciplines are interfaced quite naturally and powerfully into the Web medium as their topics, ranging from technology and sciences to the sweep of human history and art, can be brought to virtual life in instructive and beautiful new dimensions. They are freed from the static printed page. As the periodic table of elements has leapt out of books and wall charts, much of what is known by humankind is under the transformation of being interfaced in cognitively friendly new ways. Understandably the most visual studies among the disciplines have been the first to become beautiful and compelling. Astronomy, meteorology, geography, biotechnology, and earth sciences have attained new levels of online cognitive dazzle. History is enlivened by interactive timelines and digital reconstructions of physical places, like the Hippodrome at Constantinople, that no longer exist. Examples of these and other cutting-edge knowledge nuggets are listed on EdClicks.com in the section for this chapter.

In the remainder of this chapter and in the chapter that follows, I set out some thoughts on the new opportunities we now have for interfacing the study disciplines because of the Internet. The elements for expressing these disciplines through the Internet are different from those presented to the animators by the linear sequential frames. For one thing, the digital medium is dimensionless—or better said: omni-dimensional, because anything can move in any direction and can be connected with anything else and with limitless other things. This gives us a versatile new pallet of combination: anything can be made a part of anything else. This power to combine is ubiquitous in digital media because everything—text, images, sound, motion, location—is reduced to zeroes and ones that can be mixed by the media machines in limitless ways. This practical fact of digital operations has, among other wonders, completely changed video editing that used to be confined to working back and forth from reel-to-reel, winding and copying, winding and copying. Pieces of digital video can be grabbed from virtually anywhere and pasted virtually anywhere and repeated again and again—combining anything with anything in limitless dimensions. The cutting-room floor is disappearing as film morphs into zeroes and ones that require no physical support to mirror their sequencing. This escape from linear indexing is just one of many new principles that apply to available new methods of structuring and interfacing what students can learn in digital media and within its mother matrix, the Internet. The Internet, which I have depicted in figure 1.1 as a swamp, is composed of zeroes and ones that gob and glob together from the bottom up to form liquid, cans, flotsam of many sorts—some odd spots are included to suggest pornography, and, for the fun of it, a relaxing swamp frog. To begin to understand and use the new methods for exploiting the Internet toward cognitive expression, we need to look at the Internet with fresh eyes and mind.

If millions of Web pages did not already exist, and we were about to start anew to create the expressive content of the Internet, it might seem sensible to begin by separating out the different sorts of content and then establishing the best expression for each type before putting pages about them online. Instead, for half a decade we have been tossing pages by the millions into cyberspace—like those metaphoric golden cans into the swamp. What happens now? Before looking in the next chapter at the challenge of painting the big picture of study material on the Internet, it is crucial to begin at the smallest units, the individual Web page and the fundamental digital principle for expressing meaning: combination. This key principle governs the authoring of a single Web page, the growing of a Web site, the culturing of comprehensible webs within the Internet, and the formation of the mother matrix that will interface the webs of combined meaning.

Combination in nature is formation and construction from the bottom up: little pieces come together to form bigger and more complex larger parts, which in turn combine into larger entities. The combination process can be noticed in observations made by human genome projects. In every cell of our bodies, we carry a string of DNA that consists mostly of what is now described as junk. Here is how David Baltimore of the California Institute of Technology summarizes what we have learned about how many of our genes are active within the DNA substance in making us what we are:

> The sequences are about 90% complete for the euchromatic (weakly staining, gene-rich) regions of the human chromosomes. The estimated total size of the genome is 3.2 Gb (that is gigabases, the latest escalation of units needed to contain the fruits of modern technology). Of that, about 2.95 Gb is euchromatic. Only 1.1% to 1.4% is sequence that actually encodes protein; that is just 5% of the 28% of the sequence that is transcribed into RNA. Over half of the DNA consists of repeated sequences of various types: 45% in four classes of parasitic DNA elements, 3% in repeats of just a few bases, and about 5% in recent duplications of large segments of DNA.[16]

My guess is that the elegantly complex entities that exist as bacteria, fruit flies, frogs, and you and me could not have risen out of the primordial swamp without extravagant amounts of material to test and reject as well as the full liberty to be redundant without limit. The key is to combine a few selected pieces to form a combination of pieces that becomes a sum of the parts that emerges as a meaningful whole. The Internet is extravagantly memory-rich and has unlimited potential in the availability of dimensions and connectivity. During the years 1997–2001, I was watching up close as the Internet content for study disciplines quite serendipitously grew within a swamp that had become sufficiently huge to allow the formation within it of complex structures. These structures formed by the combination of selected parts into wholes which then took on meaning of their own. My last two sentences provide an opportunity to wonder: Who made the combinations in the primordial swamp that led to the emergence of life? I will resist the temptation to go there because it is not relevant to what we can learn from making the comparison that allows us to view the Internet as a primordial swamp from which we can combine elements into elegant new expressions of what students need to learn. Who made a frog and why He did it is not our subject; how we form digital cognitive objects within the golden swamp is. So we move ahead to see what instruction we can get from the method without speculation about its Author. As we will see, it is a method that appears in other instances of causing order out of chaos.

It is difficult for thoughtful people who matured in the 20th century to suppress tidying instincts. But we should quit worrying about cleaning up and organizing the golden swamp that was caused by the explosion of information that has given us millions upon millions of Web pages and lots of trouble finding them. As I mentioned earlier, it does not seem to bother our cells to be swamped by a huge amount of abandoned DNA; the cells get the information they need to make proteins by using just small parts of the coding on the string of genes. Something similar seems to have been going on when the first animals appeared on Earth. The online Museum of Paleontology from the University of California at Berkeley has a chart of the fossil record of metazoans (animals).[17] The text on the Web page with the chart explains:

> The chart above shows the oldest undoubted fossil occurrences of each of the living major groups of animals. Note how many of the animal groups have fossil records that date back to the Cambrian period, over 500 million years ago. Those groups which do not date back to the Cambrian, with the single exception of the Bryozoa, do not possess mineralized skeletons. It is likely that all major animal groups, even those which have not left us fossils, originated in the Cambrian. This sudden appearance of many major groups of animals is often referred to as the "Cambrian Explosion."

It is provocative to compare the Cambrian Explosion of animal life to the cyber explosion of Web pages during the past decade. The Paleontology Museum's exhibit includes this observation. "A few localities around the world that preserve soft-bodied fossils of the Cambrian show that the 'Cambrian radiation' generated many unusual forms not easily comparable with anything today."[18] One supposes that within not too many years many of today's Web sites will be weird relics of the era when the Internet exploded onto the scene. It is likely, says the museum, that the living results of the Cambrian Explosion of life are all the animals of our era, including you and me. Stephen Jay Gould summarized how this emergence worked: "The history of life is a story of massive removal followed by differentiation within a few surviving stocks, not the conventional tale of steadily increasing excellence, complexity, and diversity."[19] Recent studies of genes reveal that DNA still carries ancient information that is no longer used to form the living creature that carries it. These observations of nature's mechanisms for building things suggests some practical guidelines for understanding and enriching the Internet. The Internet's Cambrian Explosion has occurred, offering us a creative environment of rich multiplicity. A key method of the new expressive art we seek to invent and master is combination within that environment: to invent, assemble and interconnect forms that express what John Dewey called the organizing bodies of truth that we call studies. Doing so will begin taking us from repositioning to expressing what is known by humankind.

There are some obvious things that have to be done and corrected before the potential of the Internet for expressing human knowledge begins to be truly realized. Bandwidth has to continue to grow so downloads are faster, and richer images and animations can be used by all—this process is rapidly occurring. Where they are applicable, the lessons learned over time about cognitive information display need to be used. At the most basic level, for example, it is abhorrent to anyone with expertise in fonts and typesetting to surf through much of the Web. The fact that it is so easy to make Web pages is no excuse for breaking all the rules of aesthetics and visual literacy. Indeed it is irresponsible to degrade communication that is in effect public and available to all. The good news is that for learning to be effective from the Internet we are not faced with eliminating the mess or waiting for its mass extinction somehow to occur naturally. All we have to do is to combine and grow the good stuff for the studies and develop means by which students can find them. My guess is that like the junk genes in our cells, the lousy fonts, incomprehensible navigation bars, and (alas) the pornography will remain with us for a very long time.

As the birth of Dopey in the Disney creative nursery illustrates, in contrast to improving the repositioning of our skills from print and predigital visual media like television and cinema, there is more interesting, exciting creativity to be undertaken. I think the sort of harnessing of the new powers that took place for cartoon animation at the Disney studios in the 1930s has barely begun for digital and Internet media, particularly in the area of education. We are still using cookie cutters from older media and gluing the pieces we get onto Web pages with little rhyme or reason and just about no serious thought to artistic expression. We have a lot to learn. We are stuck in the sand for good reason: the digital and Internet media are radically different in structure from any medium we have ever encountered for knowledge communication. The greatest similarity of the new medium is to some of the principles of art. Among other things, as mentioned, the digital medium as it now occupies the Internet is omnidimensional, limitless in scope, can accept unlimited redundancy, grows from the bottom up, and can be accessed and endlessly explored by everyone on our planet. (That last part is coming very soon.) If that sounds hard to understand, well, it is. It is something like my grandpa trying to show a cavalry quartermaster sergeant how to fix a carburetor. But the new digital communication medium is wonderful, and we should apply ourselves to figuring out how to make the most of it.

Even the gifted visionary Walt Disney could not have envisioned the appearance of Dopey—that he would happen or what he might look like—in 1930. If we are at about the 1930 era in developing Internet expression, where do we begin? The most important step is, of course, to begin. I admonish the education industry to look beyond repositioning the old ways of the 20th century into the media of the 21st. Not doing so does not work well and delays a better future. But that should be obvious. Another step forward would be to follow Disney's good sense and employ people to the task who know something about expression. The tyrannies of technology and business delay expressive advance and defer profits from a yet-to-appear expressiveness of the Web, and that is clear to see. Not so obvious are the new creative principles of expression. When the talent is assembled and the goal is expression, how do we create Dopey?

Rudolf Arnheim's point about cinema gives an important clue. He explained that motion was a new tool for expression inherent in the cinema medium. I propose that the tool of combination is a fundamental key to new digital expressive power. There may be other crucial keys, but combination is a good place to begin. Whether used in print, written on a chalkboard, or positioned on Web pages, predigital materials cannot employ the incredible new digital power to form limitless combinations that interface the organizing studies, as Dewey called them. Combination is the working process in making a Web page, a Web site, and relating Web sites to each other. The most amazing aspect to me of what happens to these studies when they are formed digitally is that they seem to do their own organizing and bring with them the power to generate context. That is wonderful, and I believe bears comparison to how species arose from the Cambrian Explosion and proteins arise from the information of genes. The mechanisms are similar.

My working hypothesis, based in part on the similarities just mentioned, for how to organize ideas that are in digital form, follows. This method scales impeccably, applying equally well, as I have mentioned, to the assembling of assets for a single Web page, a Web site, and a portion of or the entire Internet. The method begins with letting go the urge to organize the whole chaotic morass from which the parts are drawn. The method, instead, starts at the level of the smallest pieces and selects only pieces that can be related to each other in meaningful ways, starting from the bottom and setting off a reaction that grows from the bottom up. While this is happening, the integrity of the pieces is preserved and they come to exist in cognitive context with other pieces of related stuff which multiplies their usefulness for learning at each level of combination. On top of that wonder, the cognitive organization of the smaller pieces leads to the emergence of groups of pieces that congeal into gestalts, where the whole new big piece is more than the sum of its parts. I suppose in the Disney studios of the 1930s such a thing, a gestalt, would be Dopey. That which makes gestalts more than the sum of their parts is that they express meaning, that the whole communicates as a thing in itself.

After the Cambrian Explosion, when creatures appeared from which virtually all living animals descended, only a few of the combinations of parts lasted and from them other animals ramified as the species branched out. In our DNA, the echoes of many abandoned ideas appear to remain. Selection from a vast swamp and meaningful combinations of the selected pieces are the working principles of both processes. Another ubiquitous example of the same method occurs in vision. From the chaos of light frequencies projected and focused on our retinas by the lenses at the front of our eyes, we construct within our visual cortex everything that we see. Capturing the light frequencies is part of seeing; the other step is the combination of the information from the frequencies into comprehensible images, or indeed any image at all. The surface of our retina is pixilated. A sea of dots is formed by thousands of nerve endings that respond to different assigned frequencies of light. A few of the points of light are selected and by combining them we construct meaning as we see a friend's face, a sunset, or the ceramic Dopey on my shelf.

Figure 5.2. A frog interfaced on paper using dots of ink.

Printers use the same principle. As you probably know, if you look at the frog in figure 5.2 with a magnifying glass you will see dots, as you will with any of the figures in this book and most printed materials. The same is true of your television screen and your computer monitor. The dots formed by the printer's screen or the cathode-ray tube's pixels are tiny enough that your eye cannot focus them individually, so they combine visually to form meaningful bigger patches—such as the frog's foot or eye. The combined patches are projected by the lenses of your eyes onto the sea of dots composed of nerve endings that form your retinas. From there, information, again broken down into dots (composed of whichever nerve endings are excited by the incoming light) is sent into your visual cortex where meaningful images arise and are experienced as seeing. By the physical structure of your retina, a printer's screen, and the surface of a cathode-ray tube, the beginning step in the method for creating a meaningful whole is to start with the littlest piece—the signal of a single nerve cell, the hole in a screen, the pixel.

Cell-building from proteins and seeing images with the eye do not occur from the top down, with a concept first and then the filling in of the contents of the protein or the picture. The opposite happens: a few molecules or firing retinal cells get together, and then that group joins with other groups consisting of a few each, building upward to fill out the protein or image. The wonder is that the total of just the right molecules or visible spots become living proteins or comprehensible images. They become gestalts. Granular implies a bunch of unattached parts. Gob refers to stuff globbed together. Gestalts are marvelously different: they are wholes that are greater than the sum of their parts. The Internet is now granular and contains a lot of gobs of knowledge pages. Gestalts are also forming through the organizing forces of the study disciplines. We are watching the spontaneous self-organization of knowledge within a new medium that offers many more dimensions to house relationships than were available in the pre-digital world. The only previous medium to compare with the Internet's omni-dimensionality is the human mind. The gestalt of dots that offers us a frog is reflected in our minds as the idea of that frog, which can then lead us to other frog thoughts. What comes to your mind when you look at the frog in figure 5.2; what mental connections jump together in your head?

The word *gestalt* means form or shape in German. Webster's dictionary defines it in English as "a structure, configuration, or pattern of physical, biological, or psychological phenomena so integrated as to constitute a functional unit with properties not derivable by summation of its parts."[20] It is the combination that causes the function, and combination is, I believe, a potent requisite tool of our new digital world; it must be our primary way of working if we are to achieve the expression that will unleash the Internet's potential for communicating the knowledge contained by the study disciplines. As motion gave new expressive energy to cinema, so combination enlivens digital expression and places us in a new theater of communication. Professor Emeritus Richard Zakia of the Rochester Institute of Technology teaches and writes about perception and imaging. In his 1997 book on the subject Professor Zakia describes the history of gestalt theory in terms that are strikingly applicable to evaluating Web pages:

> The Gestalt school of psychology, which was originated in Germany about 1912 by Dr. Max Wertheimer, provides us with some simple and convincing evidence about how man organizes and groups visual elements so that they are perceived as wholes. In other words, what you experience when you look at a picture is quite

different from what you would experience were you to look at each item in the picture separately. . . . Wertheimer might have argued that physical fields have their counterpart in psychological fields—in visual fields. The main principle of Gestalt psychology supports this; the way in which an object is perceived is determined by the total context or field in which it exists. Put differently, visual elements within a person's visual field are either attracted to each other (grouped) or repelled (not grouped).[21]

Professor Zakia goes on to say, "Photographers out to capture a picture can succeed or fail based not only on their technical or artistic competence but also on their knowledge of and sensitivity to the field in which they are working."[22]

Following Dr. Wertheimer's sequence, something physical that we see becomes something psychological that we think or learn—and it can be represented by a visual image. Painters have been excited about this idea since a human being created an image that reflected an idea back. The cave guy sees a buffalo, he paints it on the wall, he gives himself and his clan a visual expression of their thoughts. The pieces he combines on the wall include the grain of the rock and its pattern of light and dark, along with scratches and colored marks he adds. The sum of those parts becomes a visual whole: the buffalo.

The process of checking for the same sort of combining of visual elements on a typical Web page is a bit jolting. What does the banner ad have to do with the navigation bar and the two of them with some scattered images and text? Are the visual elements attracted to one another or do they repel? If the latter is the case the page is not a gestalt. But then why would that be bad? For learning and thinking the answer to that question is extremely serious: the absence of a gestalt means the absence, or at least diminution, of meaning. Without meaning there is no learning or thinking.

Another dose of confusion in Internet selection comes from the misconception that word searches are selective for ideas. As explained in an earlier chapter, they are, in fact, only selective for words as they are constructed from letters. The lists of links search engines return are also not selective for the entire Internet because their software spiders that crawl cyberspace cannot look through dynamic pages (temporarily generated by a Web site's database on command from a visitor to the site), nor do the spiders have access to many of the newest Web pages on the Internet. The most fundamental failure of search engines for using knowledge is that, even if they could locate it, they cannot perform cognitive selection and combination. People have to do that.

I believe the convention of searching the entire Internet just to find a few links is fading. The bigger and more complex the swamp, the more necessary it becomes to select just some of the pieces, combining them to build a few things. That seems to be the operating principle in the evolution of multicellular life, the construction of us from DNA, and seeing things through our eyes. You start with a zillion grains, start combining them and then combining the combinations, and a functioning or meaningful gestalt emerges. Amazing, but that is how it works. Artist Paul Klee put it this way: "Abstract formal elements are put together like numbers and letters to make concrete beings or abstract things; in the end a formal cosmos is achieved so much like creation that a mere breath suffices to transform religion into art."[23]

If you have assumed that I am theorizing and that the practical application to digital materials is speculative, you are incorrect. Quite the opposite is true. In the thick of trying to lead the organization of hundreds and then thousands of Internet links to study discipline materials, it became obvious that the only practical way to do it was from the bottom up. Education Web pages that create some categories and list in them a few recommended links have deadened research all over the Internet. The unique richness of any page or site on the Internet is not what it is, but what it combines and if and how that combination is more than the sum of the parts that have been combined. Before looking at what these parts might be on a Web page, I encourage you to take half an hour to make a dice painting to experience the emergence of a gestalt before your eyes. You may do so at EdClicks.com or by tracing the rectangle in figure 5.3 on a piece of paper and using crayon, markers, or other colors to make your painting on paper.

I thought of the dice painting years ago when I began reading the dean of gestalt aesthetic theory, Rudolf Arnheim. I was trying to learn to paint and by Arnheim was guided into exploring the intertwining of seeing and thinking. I did a number of paintings with dice myself just for the fun of watching something suddenly come to mind as the forms and colors took shape. I have used the dice painting as a project in aesthetics workshops where fascinating discussions have been provoked. I also have used the exercise with groups of children, who were always enormously enthusiastic. One little boy turned the pattern that came from his rolls of dice into a painting of a bird that belonged in a museum. The only bad result occurred when a 7-year-old girl came to me in tears to tell me she rolled yellow every single time and did not get anything but a big yellow page.

Figure 5.3. Rectangle for gestalt painting

To conjure the gestalt, follow these instructions and rules which I followed to make the two dice paintings in figure 5.4:

Draw a rectangle on a piece of paper, or trace the one provided here.
Place some numbers from 1 through 12 at marks along all four edges of the rectangle.
Roll two dice twice to connect two opposite edges using these steps:
Place a check mark next to a number on each of the opposite edges.
Write the first number you roll next to the checked spot on one of the edges.
Write the second number you roll next to the checked spot on the opposite edge.
Connect the two spots with a pencil line after rolling the dice again.
If the last number you rolled was an even number, make the line straight.
If the last number you rolled was an odd number, make the line curved.
Repeat this process until you have connected each of the two pairs of edges at least six times.
Select two, three, four, five, or six colors of markers or crayons.
Assign each color one of the numbers on one of the dice: 2 = red, 3 = lavender, and so on.
The process of connecting the sides with lines will have left the rectangle filled with random empty spaces.
Begin at the upper right corner and move across and down, back and forth, selecting one empty space at a time.
Roll one of the dice while each space is selected and color it in with the color assigned to the number you roll. If 2 = red and 3 = lavender, when you roll 2, color it red, when you roll 3, color it lavender.
When all the spaces are colored in, try to imagine meaning for some of the shapes. You may see boats or ships or faces—or just an abstract design. Feel free to add some fins or sails or an eye or nose.

If you have made your own dice painting—or if you will now imagine that you have—you will see that it is a little universe. Only the parts inside the frame are relevant. For this exercise, think of those parts as selected from an enormous swamp of possible parts and set off from the rest of the swamp by the frame. Whatever is said or is not said is caused by the parts inside the borders of the painting and their relationship to each other. This fact follows the events of the

Figure 5.4. These two dice paintings were made using the rectangle in figure 5.3 and following the rules given in this chapter. Judge them for yourself as gestalts. The painting on the left can be considered more unified, with a bird theme; how could this overall meaning be strengthened? On the right, a few fishes, perhaps a whale or two, hang together, but some pieces contribute little to a bigger picture. All pieces must contribute to the meaning for the contents within the frame to be a gestalt. Try also judging some Web pages by these criteria, for a way to look at them for meaning issuing from the combination of parts.

emergence of something alive from the primordial swamp or of a protein from the flow of nutrients we eat and send to our cells. The living animal or the functioning protein, just like the gestalt we see in our painting, are sums of parts in a relationship of function and meaning that defines them. They are no longer merely part of the chaos of random irrelevancies whence their parts came. The parts have been selected and combined. I think the first step toward making some order out of the chaos of the Internet is to select and combine, as I have said. That does not just mean spooning out some swamp water and expecting it to be useful. We must start by fishing out small pieces and combining them (along with other pieces we make and add) into meaningful wholes that are more than the sum of their parts. These gestalts, like the initial multicellular animals and the proteins derived from our DNA coding, become the building blocks at the bottom of new, larger structures we will build.

This process is, I believe, the natural and best way to create an Internet knowledge nugget. A typical example of an online exhibit built along these lines by the Chicago Historical Society is called *The Dramas of Haymarket*.[24] This Web exhibit emerges—like a protein from a nutrient swamp—from the mass of historical materials for which the society is steward. The steps in creating the exhibit must have gone something like this:

Step One. From the large collection of artifacts concerning Chicago history in the society's collections, the curators selected the best ones in their judgment to depict and document the Haymarket events of the 1880s.

Step Two. They combined the artifacts based on how they could be used to illustrate the events that took place at the Haymarket.

Step Three. They did not often combine the artifacts in more than one way. They could easily have done so by making a page combining all of the human characters, or all of the documents, for example, presenting them as pages collecting the characters or documents, and then used some of them again in other locations in the exhibit where particular pieces would have contributed to the whole.

Step Four. The pattern of the exhibit became organized around a line of time as historical collections often do.

Step Five. It is possible to enter the exhibit from several of the pages and move from any of them to related pages.

Step Six. There are two levels of pages that become fairly distinct wholes: the entry pages and the acts pages. Any parts of either can be linked as pieces to anything else within the exhibit or anywhere on the Internet!

Step Seven. The entire exhibit works as a gestalt, that is, a whole that is more than the sum of its parts: a bunch of historical artifacts are woven together in such a way that they are all part of a dramatic whole. As the introduction explains: "*The Dramas of Haymarket* itself is organized in the form of a drama, a tragedy in five Acts with a Prologue and an Epilogue."[25]

Your 20th-century mind may be mumbling that the society just decided it wanted to do a Haymarket exhibit and checked to see what they had in their archives, which would be working from the top down. Perhaps, but it seems more likely that someone came across some great artifacts and suggested they would serve as an excellent basis for an online exhibit. As you will see, some superb new materials were also prepared as the project was executed. The result was a jewel of an exhibit with many interconnected dimensions expressing the tragic events at Haymarket Square for anyone in the world to study.

Curators at the Chicago Historical Society and in the Rosetta Stone department at the British Museum did exactly the same thing: They took knowledge assets for which they were stewards and showcased them on the Internet. This sort of thing is hardly limited to the keepers of historical materials. Just about everybody who knows something is doing it. The way this trend works is another manifestation of the combining principle and of the build-from-the-bottom-up principle in digital knowledge phenomena. It is rampant. There are small gems from fascinating people like Stephen Hawking, Jane Goodall, the Dalai Lama, and the King of Jordan. Bigger ones include the U.S. Geological Survey, the Perseus Project, and the Rijksmueum. These examples take knowledge assets for which the hosts of the Web pages are the keepers and place them online. A similar and parallel trend is for enterprises with particular expertise to show visitors to their pages what they know how to do. Insurance companies describe safety procedures, tech companies show how transistors work, food companies have nutrition tutorials, and stock markets describe their operations. Web sites that are examples of these and more offerings from curators and experts can be clicked to at EdClick.com in the Expertorials section.

In chapter 4, I underlined the importance of a complete change from the need to distribute knowledge to learners in containers including books and what the thousands of knowledgeable teachers spread out through schools. There has been an incredible full reversal to the awesome ability now for all learners to imbibe knowledge from a single virtual can. I suggested you pause, pop open a soda, take some sips, and think about that great change. Something else that is different may take a while to sink in: the surfacing and interfacing of expert knowledge from within its primary sources is just as revolutionary and just as different. Have another soda and relax a bit to relish this fact: the single can from which learners are able to imbibe is filled, evaluated, and maintained by the experts who know the most about what it contains. Revolution means to go around—to come from the opposite direction—and that is exactly what is happening here. Instead of researchers for publications by the hundreds and teachers of subjects by the thousands having to go to sources to absorb knowledge to prepare it for publication and distribution, the middle step is gone. The knowledge pops up from its source directly into the virtual can that all learners share.

Over the course of the 20th century, broadcast media achieved something of the effect of a single source for distribution, but the emergence and tending of knowledge from its source is new, as is the constant availability of the knowledge. The ephemeral content of broadcast media only fleetingly inhabits time.

In the Web pages at the British Museum online where the museum's curators display and describe the Rosetta Stone there is a single metaphoric can from which anyone can imbibe the knowledge about the Rosetta Stone from the impeccable experts who are stewards of the stone. Traditions of the enormous education industry are shaken to the core by this phenomenon. The *deus ex machina* has caused a new plot to unfold. Pandora's escaped knowledge has flown back to its expert keepers. A textbook need not describe the Rosetta Stone, teachers need not prepare to retain and share knowledge about the stone—all the secondary sources are trumped by one single source.

The change in things to expecting knowledge nuggets to be put online by experts eliminates another process: the repetitive development of Web pages for a subject by people all over the country and world. When the Chicago Historical Society has produced a Web site covering the history of the events at the Haymarket, there is no expectation that the Illinois historical organization or any other maker of online historical showcases will spend creative energy and money on the Haymarket subject. Those interested in it will simply link to the exhibit at the Chicago Historical Society, combining it into any large subject such as the history of Illinois, where it would enrich the presentation. By linking to it, the Haymarket exhibits would still be a single exhibit hosted at the Chicago Historical Society, yet it could be present as a piece of several or many (unlimited) other combinations. As mentioned before, the scale of the exhibit does not increase with the number of users; regardless of the number of people who use it and the number of places that link to it, it remains a single exhibit. As the experts become masters of digital showcasing, the rest of us are relieved of having to do so. I expect that over the next months, or very few years, the knowledge experts and museums, laboratories, corporate web staffs, and academic web projects will push through to invent an expressive cognitive art that will be as engaging and durable as the animation art that gave us Dopey.

Making one word out of two—*expert* + *tutorial* = *expertorial*—I have coined a name for the Web sites that emerge from knowledge sources with pages to showcase and explain what they have and know. The trend to do this has occurred spontaneously. I believe it is snowballing into an expected practice so that its gift to school children and anyone who seeks to learn will be incalculably great. The expertorial movement comes without cost to the education establishment. Expertorials are a new opportunity for leaders and the Web staff of businesses, professions, nonprofits, unions, libraries, museums, and others who seek a way to improve education. Following the digital way and building from the bottom up, these entities begin with the expertise that is in their archives, factory, laboratory, and/or experts' heads. Including a modest allotment to their Web site budget for an expertorial and turning their creative people loose on the project puts any enterprise into the innovative new Internet knowledge expression movement.

Quite commonly, expertorials are financed out of deep pockets that pay for handsome, state-of-the-art Web sites. The growing role of Web sites that can afford excellent artistic effort is great news for the advancement of expressiveness which has been the subject of this chapter. Hopefully, the press of artistic effort to make Web pages more compelling for commerce is spilling over to include exciting, cognitively compelling knowledge nuggets from experts. To put some specific focus on what it will take to advance that expressiveness, here are three areas to consider: visual artistic expression, cognitive art, and the new expressive elements offered by digital media.

First is artistic expression. Walt Disney proved to have it right to hire the best artists he could find, and to push them to learn and invent. Usability and navigation are secondary to expression. So long as the first two continue to reign, expression is stunted. There is a saying among painters that good structure (in a painting) does not show. Usability and navigation are structure and should not show. Once I took a young nephew of mine to see the Rembrandts that I worship at the Metropolitan Museum of Art. He said he did not like the portraits because they were too realistic. My nephew had a good eye. He completely captured the master's vision, but he was not seeing anything that was real. The expressive power of a Rembrandt portrait is so overwhelming that you have to mask the big canvas and examine a couple of isolated inches to see that nothing is there but a jumble of spots and streaks of color. Criticizing a navigation bar by holding it up to a Rembrandt is extreme, but the point is valid. Few "nav" bars are comprehensible visually; most are lists of words, and many are made hard to read by meaningless spots and streaks of color. If you do not understand something visually, you have to stop, read it, and try to follow what you understand from the meaning of the words.

Over thousands of years artists have acquired methods and tools that express and communicate. From the prehistoric cave artists to the inventive geniuses of ancient civilizations along rivers and bountiful in forests, to classical explosions of ideas in Asia and Greece, to renaissances experienced in later civilizations, and to modern ideas yet to be tested by time, there are principles that communicate through art. Slow download times have excused ignoring the wisdom of the generations, but that day is fading fast. Internet artistic expression is waiting for a Disney-type studio to invent it. Whoever does that stands to win great fame and fortune, as Walt Disney did. Later today, when I walk down Second Avenue near my studio, I will pass a bus shelter at 83rd Street where a giant ad is posted for the new Disney DVD of *Snow White and the Seven Dwarfs*. The ad features a large, grinning picture of Dopey, who is still hugely profitable for his owners. Dopey is a piece of art that for more than six decades has fulfilled the company goal at Disney: to make people happy. Artistic expression is achieved on a Web site when what we perceive and experience from it radiates its goal as Dopey does for Disney.

Second is cognitive art. Artistic expression is experienced without or beyond words, making words difficult to use in describing it. Cognitive art is easier to explore with words. It deals with the intimacy of our senses and our thoughts—the relationship between sights, sounds, and other sensual input to thinking. Cognitive art seems to be more accessible to those of us who do not have a significant artistic gift than is the production of artistic expression.

As you may have guessed, I have done a lot of reading about art and aesthetics. I started doing so because I wanted to learn to paint. Soon I realized that before I could paint, I had to learn to draw. My shelves are crowded with books on how to draw dogs, cats, trees, and people, and how to paint with watercolor, acrylics, and oils. All these books provide examples to copy, but they do not get to the underlying understanding that leads to the power to draw or paint one's own dog or watercolor. My experience in classes has been similar: I learned to paint the way the teacher painted. Frustrated but persistent, I began a thorough investigation of the methods of the great painters, but that gave me neither a fundamental understanding of the visual arts nor the power to draw or paint from my own perception. Rudolf Arnheim's explanations of gestalts and Kimon Nicolaides's explanations of gesture opened the way to getting a handle on some of it, and I learned a lot that I think can and should be applied to authoring Web sites. I suppose much of that understanding is what a gifted artist knows intuitively, but without the gift it became for me an intellectual pursuit. I still cannot paint well, but I think I have a pretty good idea what it involves. Since both have the same goal of expression, they are highly relevant to the challenge of making Web sites communicate.

Visual gestalt and gesture are very close to the same thing: they are what the visual field is doing, and thus what it communicates. In describing the gesture drawing, which Nicolaides prescribed by the hundreds as practice for learning to see, that master teacher said:

> You should draw not what it looks like, not even what it is, but what the thing is *doing*. Feel how the figure lifts or droops—pushes forward here—pulls back there—pushes out here—drops down easily there. Suppose that the model takes the pose of a fighter with fists clenched and jaw thrust forward angrily. Try to draw the actual *thrust* of the jaw, the *clenching* of the hand. A drawing of prize fighters should show the push, from foot to fist, behind their blows that makes them hurt. [italics Nicolaides'][26]

Kimon Nicolaides was teaching drawing and painting at the Art Students League in New York City during the years that the Disney artists were elevating cartoon animation and giving birth to Dopey. When Nicolaides died in 1938, former students assisted in the completion of the draft of his book, *The Natural Way to Draw*,[27] and it was published in 1941. Sixty years later the book remains in print and it has been for all those years a standard guide for learning to draw. Its ranking of number sales among the hundreds of thousands of books listed on Amazon.com was 3,821 in October 2001, reflecting in part its popularity with the large new generation of digital animation artists. Nicolaides lived before science figured out that what we see through our eyes is interpreted by our minds by making images from the pixels of firing nerve endings on our retinas. He did observe from his experience as a teacher that: "A man can usually draw the thing he knows best whether he is an artist or not. A golfer can draw a golf club, a yachtsman can make an intelligible drawing of a sail."[28] Art is quite fundamentally cognitive, here for the golfer and yachtsman expressing what they know.

Richard Zakia paid tribute to Rudolf Arnheim with this dedication of his book that I quoted from earlier: "To Professor Rudolf Arnheim, a dear friend, colleague, and mentor who has kept the spirit of Gestalt perception alive in the 20th century."[29] One of Arnheim's books is titled *Visual Thinking*.[30] His title sums up our discussion. Cognitive art is about how the artifact is involved with thinking. Learning happens when the student gets it—when an idea that comes from the outside pops up in her head. In authoring knowledge nugget Web pages we should use the powers of cognitive art to stimulate visual thinking. As the little girl in figure 5.5 clicks around and through Web pages her experience should be cognitive: she should be thinking and learning. The Internet facilitates her thinking because, like seeing and like thinking, the web medium combines things to create meaning. The essence of the Internet is to combine things, yet how seldom so far do the Web pages we experience harness this new power of combination to create significant meaning. They usually are pages of text to read with an image or two, a navigation bar, and other distractions from whatever central point might be communicated. The whole is seldom more than the sum of the parts. I accept the admonition by Leonardo da Vinci from the first page of Nicolaides' book: "The supreme misfortune is when theory outstrips performance." But I do not think it is overly theoretical to insist that we work to find and to master the cognitive art potential of Web pages. To do so will be a gift of enormous value to education.

Third, we need to consider the new expressive elements of digital media. Some of the new elements are mixed in with older ones discussed above, just as there would be no way to fully separate the dwarf Dopey from the fellow in the Grimm Brothers story who was the seventh unnamed dwarf. Also, the fundamental new expressive element of combination has crept into the discussion above because it is ubiquitous in the subject of web function, authoring, and design. Before considering specific steps for working with new expressive elements, it is also useful to appreciate once again that access has swamped us: it has laid before anyone and everyone everything we ever knew to be linked in any conceivable dimension. The unfolding story of the 21st century is how we cope with and take advantage of this entirely new status of human knowledge. Personal communication, business, government, entertainment, and other areas are affected and forever changed. Education is changing as well. The substance of the study disciplines already resides in cyberspace. Making it more useful includes making the Internet medium more expressive of the knowledge it interfaces.

When I first began developing the project at HomeworkHeaven.com in 1997, I came across the work of Anniina Jokinen. Her Web site *Luminarium.org* has continued through the ensuing years and remains one of the finest sources for the humanities on the Internet. She does the Web site on her own for the joy

Figure 5.5.   Handheld knowledge.

of it, and not for financial profit. Here is this intellectual leader of the Internet's insight into expression through her new medium:

> I wanted the site to be a multimedia experience in the [literary] periods. I find it easier to visualize what I am reading when there is a small illustration or a tidbit about the background of the author or his work. The music and art of the period complement one's rational experience of the site with the emotional. There are people who write to me who seem to think that if something has a beautiful wrapping, it cannot possibly have scholarly insides. But I do not see why something scholarly cannot at the same time be attractive. It is that marriage of form and function, so celebrated during the Renaissance, for which my site strives.[31]

Kudos to Ms. Jokinen for seeking expressive beauty in the combination of great words, contemporary music (audio files that play from her Web pages), and handsome visuals. She follows in the tradition of Winsor McCay creating Gertie the Dinosaur before cartoon animation expressiveness was appreciated. Jokinen was ahead of her time, and still is. I believe she gives us a peek at a future I cannot predict. The appearance and operation of an Internet in which the subjects of academic study will be interfaced with the powerful new tools of digital authoring is unseen, just as Dopey was in the early 1930s, even by those who would create him. Instead it is productive to define the new tools and work toward a procedure in which expressiveness and communication of knowledge are the primary goals. I have these guidelines to suggest:

The first guideline is choice and focus. The inclination to organize the entire swamp, or even areas of it, will prove futile. Within the morass are discrete ingredients that can be used; the rest can be ignored.

The second guideline is to choose the same piece over and over. Astoundingly, every piece can be used redundantly without limit: You do not place a piece in the best place, you place it every place it adds to the meaning. That is new in information media. You cannot do this in a library, or in print. We do, however, do exactly that in concept forming in our minds. As a frivolous example, you have a concept of a mouse. Effortlessly, you can use that concept in a thought about a cat toy, a kitchen invader, a hat with ears, or a lab animal. Each context leads to other thoughts. Digital knowledge nuggets are like that, too.

The third guideline is to pick media tools that are the most expressive of the message. The Internet offers most of the old expressive tools: text, images, motion, and sound. It offers new ones too: interactivity, connectivity, nonlinearity, and more. Use the tools that best express the meaning inherent in what you seek to convey. Just as using the technical toys just because they are there and cool makes no expressive sense, using an expressive tool for the same reason accomplishes nothing either. Use the tool or combination of tools that best conveys the meaning of the subject. There is no reason to use any other tools, unless you have gotten sidetracked into showing off how cool the tool is. If text says it best, just use text. If the combination of all the tools makes the topic compelling and clear, use them all. Following are some examples of study discipline topics that are particularly enhanced by each of the tools mentioned here, and can be accessed online through the EdClick.com pages.

Text: E-books
Images: Art and astronomy
Motion: Growth of a fetus
Sound: Language pronunciation
Interactivity: Tables of periodic elements
Connectivity: Live cams
Nonlinearity: Maps

The fourth guideline is to build from the inside out, from the bottom up. (Don't think this is easy—it is very new and counterintuitive for most people who have a gift for organization.) Build assets from little parts to make bigger parts with scrupulous cognitive integrity. Start with the smallest bits, put them together into bigger pieces, and put these together into larger wholes. In the manner that your body makes molecules, puts them together into proteins, and these form and cause diverse large pieces of what becomes you (the whole), you should make little digital representations of facts, put them together into bigger concepts, and put these together into whole ideas. This, unfortunately, happens very seldom with study discipline assets on the Internet—and that is in interesting contrast to e-commerce where powerful Web sites have been assembled from myriad specialized units. On the study discipline side you are likely to encounter whole lists of links, on chemistry, or engineering, or archaeology, where you click in from a top page and rapidly come to the end of a thread somewhere out in cyberspace. E-commerce includes investment, banking, travel, other businesses where the Web site is a configuration of small functioning units from which you can work laterally, inward, and outward to useful related parts of the Web site, and that serve different types of customers and products. In the latter e-commerce examples, the whole Web site is a powerful sum of the configured parts.

The fifth guideline is to allow and encourage the natural formation of context. Because of the rich interlinking on the Internet, context will create itself if you give it half a chance. (More about that in the next chapter.)

The sixth guideline is to pay attention to the harmony and value of the cyberscape. We need to move beyond constructing portals and gateways and begin creating pavilions, parks, and fairs where exhibits are planned among pleasant pathways. (The next chapter elaborates.)

Beyond analysis, theory, and practical considerations there is a pragmatic, simple bottom line to the new power of combining that has come to us in digital technologies: you cannot just combine anything with anything. Although a lot of Web pages and Web sites do exactly that, they have not really combined anything and their parts repel each other. Combinations that do not make sense are nonsense. After the Cambrian Explosion, combinations of parts that formed critters who could not defend themselves went extinct. In our DNA, the wrong combination causes genetic disorders that halt maturation or cause disability and usually prevent reproduction. Pieces have to combine in particular ways for gestalts to emerge as viable wholes, and if they do not do so what emerges is dysfunctional, or nothing. For a rule of thumb to evaluate Web pages use this one: combinations that do not make sense are nonsense. You will see that nonsense is also neither expressive nor beautiful.

The digital power of combination—the fundamental operative of the digital world, and thus the Internet—is a potent solution for a long-standing difficulty in organized education: the fractured, piecemeal, mixed-up nature of the knowledge that children have tended to experience as they have made their way through 20th century schools. It is my considered view that repositioning most pre-Internet types of learning materials onto the Internet simply makes them available. It does not enhance them, and often they do not work as well as they did in hardcopy. A vexing problem from repositioning of curriculum from the past is the worsening effect it has on pulling apart combinations of facts and ripping subjects from their context to offer them in a sterile isolation. Piecemeal, selected, and watered-down offerings of subject matter are a necessary evil in the publication of printed textbooks and curricula, but they are sad to see in the Internet environment in which combination is a potent tool of communication, and where rich context occurs naturally. We will discuss this latter point in more detail in the next chapter.

As motion was elementary to cinematography and caused changes from the past and invention of new forms of expression, so the combining nature of digital creativity is offering—and indeed forcing—exciting new approaches to the formation of educational material. The new digital matrixing of studies is causing us to structure the materials from which we learn them in ways much closer to the cognitive structure of the topics themselves and to provide anyone who wants to learn a subject with natural routes by which to explore study disciplines from their simplest to their most complex. In figure 5.6 a ruler marks the rough, general stages from simple to complex for the subject of cell biology on the left. On the right is the K–12 sequence of school grades a student traditionally progresses through. Throughout the 20th century a large industry of curriculum writers and school administrators spent their energies taking pieces of the subjects like cell biology, and of all study disciplines, from the figurative left side of the ruler and inserting them where they deemed appropriate on the right side of the ruler. The sequence and relationship between the parts of cell biology and

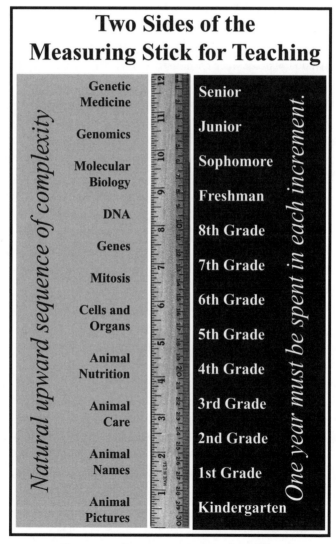

Figure 5.6.   Two ways to organize knowledge.

other subjects that kids encountered was experienced as pieces popping up here and there through their school years. There are many parts to cell biology that are interrelated in particular ways, but the whole that results from those relationships may never occur to or be experienced by most students.

The Internet, like the left side of the ruler, naturally interfaces study disciplines as wholes, with the simple and elementary pages leading to more complex, and from there out to the edge of emerging research and knowledge. Not so on the right: a chapter in a fourth-grade textbook about animal nutrition has no bridge for the precocious kid to move out to learn a topic assigned to a later grade, like how the nutrition assists in the growth of cells and organs. Conversely, the sixth-grader stuck in mitosis with no clue about cell basics is linked to no bridge back to fundamentals he should have learned in the third grade. On the Internet the internal structures of subjects themselves can design the combinations of images, text, and navigation paths of the study disciplines: genomics is weblike, history is linear and links abound to the next related ideas. The Internet is solving the intellectual piecemealing that has been imposed by a system of education divided into pieces of grades and materials. Education itself promises to be reborn as a golden global gestalt. But first there is a lot of combining to do and context to showcase. Please turn to the next chapter and meet me in Saint Louis.

NOTES

1. Frank Thomas and Ollie Johnston, *Disney Animation: The Illusion of Life* (New York: Abbeville Press, 1981), 27.

2. *The Complete History of the Discovery of Cinematography*, www.precinemahistory. net/index.html [accessed 6 August 2001].

3. *Digital Media FX*, "The History of Animation: Advantages and Disadvantages of the Studio System in the Production of an Art Form," www.digitalmediafx.com/Features/ animationhistory.html [accessed 7 August 2001].

4. David Siegel, *Creating Killer Web Sites* (Indianapolis: Hayden Books, 1996), xv.

5. Jakob Nielsen, *Designing Web Usability* (Indianapolis: New Riders, 2000), 9.

6. Nielsen, *Designing Web Usability*, 99.

7. Thomas and Johnston, *Disney Animation*, 73.

8. Jef Raskin, *The Humane Interface* (Boston: Addison-Wesley, 2000), frontispiece.

9. Raskin, *The Humane Interface*, 1.

10. Thomas and Johnston, *Disney Animation,* 23.

11. Thomas and Johnston, *Disney Animation,* 25.

12. *Merriam-Webster's Collegiate Dictionary,* 10th ed. (Springfield, Mass.: Merriam-Webster, 1997.)

13. *All Family Resources, Grimms Fairy Tales,* www.familymanagement.com/literacy/grimms/grimms42.html [accessed 11 October 2001].

14. Rudolf Arnheim, *Film as Art* (Berkeley: University of California Press, 1957), 181–82.

15. John Canemaker, *Paper Dreams: The Art & Artists of Disney Storyboards* (New York: Hyperion, 1999), 115.

16. David Baltimore, "Our Genome Unveiled," *Nature: News & Views,* www.nature.com/cgi-taf/DynaPage.taf?file=/nature/journal/v409/n6822/full/409814a0_fs.html [accessed 9 August 2001].

17. *Museum of Paleontology,* "Metazoa: Fossil Record," www.ucmp.berkeley.edu/phyla/metazoafr.html [accessed 9 August 2001].

18. *Museum of Paleontology,* "Life During the Cambrian Period," www.ucmp.berkeley.edu/cambrian/camblife.html [accessed 9 August 2001].

19. Stephen Jay Gould, *Wonderful Life* (New York: W.W. Norton, 1989), 25.

20. *Merriam-Webster's Collegiate Dictionary,* 1997.

21. Richard D. Zakia, *Perception and Imaging* (Boston: Focal Press, 1997), 30.

22. Zakia, *Perception and Imaging,* 31.

23. Zakia, *Perception and Imaging,* 29.

24. *Chicago Historical Society,* "The Dramas of Haymarket," www.chicagohs.org/dramas/index.htm [accessed 23 July 2001].

25. *Chicago Historical Society,* "The Dramas of Haymarket."

26. Kimon Nicolaides, *The Natural Way to Draw* (Boston: Houghton Mifflin, 1941), 15.

27. Nicolaides, *The Natural Way to Draw,* 15.

28. Nicolaides, *The Natural Way to Draw,* 6.

29. Zakia, *Perception and Imaging,* dedication.

30. Rudolf Arnheim, *Visual Thinking* (Berkeley: University of California Press, 1969), title.

31. Anniina Jokinen, *Luminarium,* www.luminarium.org/letter.htm [accessed 11 August 2001].

6

THE NEW WORLD'S FAIR OF USEFUL KNOWLEDGE

Meet Me in Saint Louis

In December 1803, the expeditionary band led by Meriwether Lewis and William Clark encamped on the Illinois side of the Mississippi River opposite the point where the Missouri River flowed in from the west. They established a winter camp, which they occupied until the following May when they departed to follow the Missouri upriver to explore America's new West and to seek a route to the Pacific Ocean. Nearly two centuries had passed since Henry Hudson let the wind push him north up the river that bears his name. Once they had floated down the Ohio from Pittsburgh to the Mississippi, river transportation for the Lewis and Clark expeditionary force for the remainder of their travels west was usually powered by human muscles, rowing and dragging their boats against strong currents that often made their progress painfully slow. Now and then, when the wind was to their backs, the sail could be raised on the large keel boat, but mainly it was row and push. Back east, Robert Fulton was working on his steamboat, but its key role in midwest transport was in the future. Stephen Ambrose, in his biography of Meriwether Lewis, describes the primitive transportation that isolated the young American republic land beyond the Appalachians:

> To the west, beyond the mountains, there were no roads at all, only trails. To move men or mail from the Mississippi River to the Atlantic Seaboard took six weeks or more; anything heavier than a letter took two months at least. . . . People took it for

granted that things would always be this way. The idea of progress based on techno-logical improvements or mechanics, the notion of a power source other than muscle, falling water, or wind, was utterly alien to virtually every American. Writing in the last decade of the nineteenth century about conditions in the year of Jefferson's inaugural, Henry Adams observed that "great as were the material obstacles in the path of the United States, the greatest obstacle of all was in the human mind. Down to the close of the eighteenth century no change had occurred in the world which warranted prac-tical men in assuming great changes were to come."[1]

Still, the American Enlightenment was stirring as centers of culture and so-phistication were growing. The great philosopher president Thomas Jefferson was in the White House and future education pioneers Mary Lyon and Horace Mann were kindergarten age. The American Philosophical Society, founded by Benjamin Franklin in 1843, encouraged the pursuit of what the members termed useful knowledge. Before sending him to explore the West, Jefferson sent Meri-wether Lewis to Philadelphia to be trained by some of the society's members, and by other naturalists and geographers. While the Lewis and Clark expedition had important political and economic implications for the United States—as the Louisiana Purchase in 1803 had extended the nation over vast wilderness to the virtually unknown Rocky Mountains—the grand mind of Jefferson attached high importance in the first westward exploration to acquiring useful knowledge.

In describing the Internet as a golden swamp, and elsewhere in this book, I have referred to the cascade of the study disciplines, as John Dewey called them, into cyberspace. I believe the substance of these disciplines—that which makes the cyber swamp golden—is what Franklin, Jefferson, and other 18th-century philosophers meant by useful knowledge. The American Philosophical Society Web site provides an explanation of the quest for this sort of knowledge that mo-tivated the society's founding and continues as its central theme:

"The first drudgery of settling new colonies is now pretty well over," wrote Benjamin Franklin in 1743, "and there are many in every province in circumstances that set them at ease, and afford leisure to cultivate the finer arts, and improve the common stock of knowledge." The scholarly society he advocated became a reality that year. By 1769 international acclaim for its accomplishments assured its permanence. Franklin's influence and the needs of American settlements led the Society in its early days to pursue equally "all philosophical Experiments that let Light into the Nature of Things, tend to increase the Power of Man over Matter, and multiply the Conveniences or Pleasures of Life." Early members included doctors, lawyers, clergymen, and merchants interested in science, and also many learned artisans and tradesmen like Franklin. Many founders of the republic were members: George Washington, John Adams, Thomas Jefferson, Alexander Hamilton, Thomas Paine, Benjamin Rush, James Madison, and John Marshall; as were many distinguished foreigners: Lafayette, von Steuben, Kosciusko.[2]

The American struggle for freedom and liberty was either blessed by the co-incidence of many geniuses or its fever enticed genius where it might have lain dormant. Perhaps there was a combination of both factors. Many who have studied the era single out Jefferson as the superstar. President John Kennedy summed it up in 1962, after hosting a dinner at the White House for 49 Nobel prize winners, including scientists, authors, composers, and artists. JFK said he had been in the company of the most "extraordinary collection of talent, of human knowledge that has ever been gathered together at the White House with the possible exception of when Thomas Jefferson dined alone."

Meriwether Lewis undertook the leadership of the exploratory expedition to the western wilderness after intense personal preparation by Jefferson during a stint when Lewis served as secretary to the president. Jefferson was a widower. Lewis, who was unmarried, had been an army officer for several years, assigned to several posts and traveling extensively. He seldom visited the plantation in Virginia that he owned and which was managed by his widowed mother and his younger siblings. When Lewis came to Washington to take the secretarial job with Jefferson, he moved into the White House with quarters in what is now the East Room. He lived there for the next two years until departing to organize and then lead the western exploration. He worked for the president on the nation's business, dined with him, usually joined by interesting and important guests, and spent vacations with him at Monticello.

During the winter of 1803–04 William Clark spent most of his time across the Mississippi from Saint Louis in the expedition's camp. He supervised and trained the men and worked with them to ready the equipment for the trip. Lewis was doing other expedition business—procuring supplies, maps, and information—for the majority of that time, in Saint Louis. There were then a little more than a thousand residents in Saint Louis. The original log houses of the 40-year-old town were being replaced by frame houses, but no bricks had yet been made. No streets were paved. Saint Louis was a commercial town that handled fur trade from the West. Everyone knew change was coming. Jefferson had cut the deal in 1803 with Napoleon to purchase the Louisiana Territory for the United States. On 8–9 March 1804, Lewis served as official witness to the ceremonies in front of the Saint Louis Government House for the formal transfer of Upper Louisiana from Spain to France, and then from France to the United States. Tenuous, temporary, and conflicting claims to the lands involved had continued through the 17th and 18th centuries among the Spanish, French, British, and even the Russians in the northwest. Occupying the distant land in mid-continent just did not happen for any of them. But the Americans were now poised to pour over the eastern mountains to claim and tame the wild west. For the native Americans who already lived there, disease and disruption came as well.

The inquiring minds of the American Enlightenment and the exploring energies of those who first penetrated the American West took the big-picture approach. The organizational urge to put all the parts into a meaningful whole was the guiding worldview of the times. Such is the goal of scientific inquiry itself: to understand how reality works. Reality was conceived as the pattern into which things fit. (A century later when quantum mechanics undermined the certainty that everything could be understood, Albert Einstein responded that it was his opinion that God did not do things that way: "The [quantum] theory says a lot, but does not really bring us closer to the secret of the 'Old One.' I, at any rate, am convinced that He is not playing at dice."[3] In the heyday of the enlightened science of Jefferson's era, the operational approach was that if a hypothesis or formula did not prove to work in every instance, the hypothesis was judged to be wrong and it was discarded and the search continued for a hypothesis that did fit. Approaching the vast lands of the Louisiana Purchase in a parallel spirit, what lay before the inquirers of 1804 was the sketching in of geography, natural resources, economic potential, and practicalities of settlement—all to be filled in and acted on to understand and define the new land. I imagine that it would never have crossed the minds of the 18th-century members of the American Philosophical Society or to Lewis and Clark to doubt that useful knowledge could ultimately be acquired in full by humankind or that the land west of the Mississippi could be completely explored and tamed. God did not roll dice. Perhaps that view underlay the assumption Henry Adams described that great changes were not going to come. In the latter part of the 20th-century it was not just the physicists who had to deal with incomplete descriptions of reality. Chaos theory began to demonstrate that it was possible not to see a big picture if it is too large and complex. There can be just too much information for it all (at least so far) to be captured and understood in meaningful order. Forecasting next month's weather is like that because it would be based on every known trend in every sector of our planet's atmosphere with so many different possible combinations of winds, storms, calms, and moisture patterns that predicting the one combination that really will occur is impossible. As the Internet has become enormous, it takes on the character of that sort of chaos. At every level, digital content does this same thing. Certainly it has done so on my hard drive—that is to say my several hard drives. I have two main ones now slotted into my box plus unlimited possible smaller ones that I could use by plugging them into my system. Ten years ago, I could tell you everything contained in my computer. Now I just have a general idea what is there, along with several strategies for finding files. My computer's content reached the stage of semichaos when I began acquiring storage by the gigabyte. Now that I have more than 30 gigs, it is truly chaotic because there is ample memory for me to quit worrying from a storage point of view about trashing things that I no longer need. In addition to that source of junk, when I load new software programs, most of what is placed in my hard drives is stuff I will never use. I have, for example, a spreadsheet program which I use for very little else than to make simple listings for my taxes, while powerhouse features for accounting and graphical reporting lie idle among my gigabytes. By now, I suppose many more of the files stored in my hard drives are obsolete or unneeded than are pertinent. Soon my computer memory will be like my DNA, with barely any of it in use.

The subject of this chapter is how to organize and interface what is contained by the Internet—or my hard drives, or any thriving digital repository of content. I think the best formula is the same as I provided in the preceding chapter for organizing a single piece of expressive cognitive content: select, then combine, and context will emerge. In this chapter, we approach the process from the end result: context. Intriguingly, context—which is ever-shifting as we move within it—may be as close as we can get to a big picture of meaning within a digital setting. Before looking at context as it emerges from the Internet, some predigital examples of its beauty and educational importance can be seen by taking a look at the great Saint Louis World's Fair of 1904 and the 19th-century invention of landscape architecture that led to the physical arrangement of the fair.

A publication at the time of the fair captures its importance and the enthusiasm that abounded for the great event:

The World's Fair of 1904 celebrates the Centennial of the Louisiana Purchase, an event in American history having an importance secondary only to the Declaration of Independence. The territory acquired from France by this purchase embraced all the land lying between the Mississippi river and the crest of the Rocky Mountains, and its ownership by the United States made possible the extension of the nation's boundaries to the Pacific Ocean. No centennial was ever so grandly celebrated, for this Exposition is without a peer in history, and a visit within its gates is an event to be always remembered with pleasure and satisfaction by young and old alike.[4]

Another contemporary description applauds the magnificent vistas that were a major attraction, along with the fun to be had:

It has been remarked that at previous expositions there were but two or three good views, while the Louisiana Purchase Exposition has hundreds. Of these the prospect from Festival Hall over the Grand Basin ranks easily among the first. Here one has the glorious stretch of water, with its surface gently rippled by passing gondolas and launches, and all the way down the lagoon and along the Plaza of St. Louis are rows of transplanted maple trees, affording shade and the color of verdure. To the right lies the stately Palace of Education, with the Manufactures Palace beyond it. To the left, crowned by figures holding aloft golden stars, is Electricity Palace, and further along the Palace of Varied Industries. Fronting the Grand Basin is the tall Louisiana Purchase Monument, torched with gold. On beyond is the broad Plaza, with level space for multitudes. At right and left are band-stands and statuary, and in the center line is the heroic figure of King Louis IX of France, the great Crusader and patron saint of the City of St. Louis. In the far distance are the Tyrolean Alps, a fitting background. At sunset is perhaps the best time to see this view, when the dying lights soften and mellow every object. Then the view is enchanting. A little later, when the myriad lights show forth, and the cascades play, it is entrancing.[5]

We can look at the 1904 World's Fair as a terrific place to have fun: to dance the *Hoochee Koochee* with your tootsie wootsie, however the *Hoochee Koochee* was danced at the time all across the land. The fair was certainly worth visiting just to see the vistas, but there was another very different attraction. In 1904, before radio, movies, television, and air travel, the chance to see the most up-to-date useful knowledge was compelling. The fair was a fine opportunity to take in exhibits at the edge of what was known, to see what was being done in many fields, and view objects and traditions from and about many parts of the United States and of the world. The useful knowledge to be encountered at the fair was pavil-

ioned in magnificent palaces erected in a beautiful park featuring gracious pathways and comforts for the visitor. The effect was to set each piece of knowledge
into context and make it intuitively accessible as visitors wandered through the
palaces. All these characteristics make the fair a fine metaphor for the intellectual
Internet that is now forming in cyberspace.

One century after Lewis and Clark started out from the small river town with
their expedition up the Missouri, Saint Louis's population exceeded 575,000
and 20 million people visited the city to attend the World's Fair that celebrated
the centennial of the Louisiana Purchase. "Don't tell me the lights are shining
anywhere but there," proclaimed the most popular song of 1904: *Meet Me in
Saint Louis, Louis*. Lights, yes; in fact there was an entire Palace of Electricity
adorned with thousands of bulbs and housing exhibits on home lighting, X-ray
use in medicine, electrochemistry, and other advances. "Ding, ding, ding went
the trolley," goes another lyric that captures the times. By 1904, Saint Louis had
had used trolleys for more than 50 years. The fair included a Palace of Transportation. One of the excellent Web sites dedicated to the 1904 World's Fair
gives these details on the transportation exhibits:

> The historical display of old locomotives showed graphically the long struggle from
> the time of the stage coach to the era of the modern palace car. Visitors were permit-
> ted to inspect the most palatial trains. A huge locomotive stood in the center of the
> building upon a turn-table. In the western end of the building was a laboratory for
> testing the efficiency of locomotives. The old horse car and the modern trolley car
> stood side by side. The display of automobiles showed the remarkable possibilities
> of this new means of travel. Motor boats and other water craft were here in good num-
> bers while the road vehicles for all sorts of purposes were not forgotten. Models of
> railway stations, cars and other railway equipment were displayed.[6]

The palace images in figures 6.1 and 6.2 are from postcards mailed to my father's parents from Saint Louis during the fair. The postmark is 1904, the stamp
1 cent, and the address simply Dr. L. M. Breck, El Paso, Texas. My grandfather
Breck was El Paso's third dentist, practicing through the first three decades of
the 20th century. The city was an important crossroads, the division point to the
Midwest and South for the transcontinental railroad from California that arrived
there in 1881, and was located at the Pass of the North through the desert mountains on the centuries-old north–south route to Santa Fe from the interior of
Mexico.

Meet me in Saint Louis, Louis, Meet me at the fair.
Don't tell me the lights are shining, Any place but there.
We will dance the Hoochee Koochee, I will be your tootsie wootsie;
Meet me in Saint Louis, Louis, Meet me at the fair.

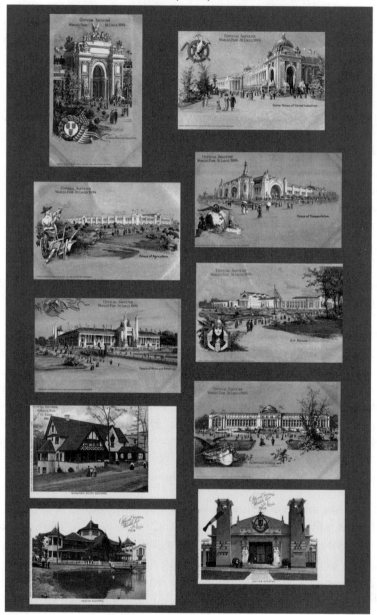

Figure 6.1.   Postcards sent to Dr. L. M. Breck in 1904 from the Saint Louis World's Fair. A sampling of the palaces (clockwise, from top left): Liberal Arts, Varied Industries, Transportation, Art, Government, Austria, Ceylon, Wisconsin, Mines and Metallurgy, and Agriculture. Visit the EdClicks.com Knowledge Fair for online collections echoing subjects these palaces displayed.

Figure 6.2.   Palace of Transportation

Figure 6.3.   Dr. Louis M. Breck at the wheel of his 1905 Pope Toledo. It was the 17th licensed automobile in El Paso, Texas.

When Lewis and Clark were in Saint Louis in 1803–04, it would have taken months to have posted a message from there to the Spanish Missions then active along the Rio Grande at the Pass of the North. To have ridden by horseback west from Saint Louis to that river valley would have been possible, but arduous and dangerous. Meriwether Lewis had given President Jefferson great concern by sending him a letter before reaching the Mississippi saying he planned to ride to Santa Fe, north of the El Paso area about 300 miles, while the expedition waited out the winter at Saint Louis. The press of expedition business caused Lewis to abandon the idea, although it was many weeks before the worried president's letter arrived to order Lewis not to take the ride. Transportation was safe, comfortable—even genteel—and very much faster by the time throngs were meeting at the fair in Saint Louis. The year before it opened, my mother's grandmother, Julia E. Spaulding, set out alone by train from Independence, Missouri, 250 miles west of Saint Louis, to move to the West Coast. She kept a diary of her trip, which lasted five days (it took Lewis and Clark two years!) beginning on 27 November 1903. The first evening, she wrote something of her fellow travelers:

> I was nicely settled in my surroundings. Across from me was a family of four, a middle aged gentleman and wife, a young man of about 20 and a little boy of 3 years. The woman dressed in a bright blue wool wrapper was very motherly looking and after some conversation, found they were from Indiana and had made several trips to Cal. The little boy was an orphan grandchild. The dear little fellow went to bed almost as soon as we left K.C. The people in no. 4 area, a jolly set, were playing cards all the eve.[7]

Within a little more than a decade, Julia's son-in-law would be outfitting a shop in a railroad car in New Mexico to repair General Pershing's motor vehicles where they were getting stuck in the sand. Many things, and most certainly transportation, had been radically improved from the travel conditions experienced a century earlier by Lewis and Clark. Although Henry Adams thought people alive in 1804 could not have imagined such changes, my guess is that Franklin, Jefferson, and probably Lewis, would have expected them. In any event, the technological transformation of the 19th century is a powerful example of the possibility of change and progress.

We must not have the mind-set about education that Henry Adams described, where fundamental change is not expected. We owe more than that to future generations. The focus and theme of the 1904 Saint Louis World's Fair was to provide a showcase for useful knowledge for the world to visit. It is my fervent hope and informed expectation that a great new fair, pavilioning useful knowledge, is arising on the Internet to transform learning everywhere. The 1904 World's Fair was the biggest and most successful event of its kind ever held—before or since. Its magnificent palaces were dedicated to major fields of useful knowledge: Agriculture, Education and Social Economy, Electricity and Machinery, Horticulture, Liberal Arts, Machinery, Manufactures, Mines and Metallurgy, Transportation, and Varied Industries. More than 40 states and territories erected buildings on the fair grounds to house exhibits, wares, plants, and other products and objects of pride. More than 40 foreign countries did the same. The fair also boasted an elaborate pike, to be strolled to enjoy shows, games, and other amusements. The Festival Hall and Central Cascades, Administration, and other buildings capped the magnificence that magnetized Saint Louis and attracted the millions of visitors.

Frederick Law Olmsted died in 1903. He had been ill and not active for most of the decade before his death, yet his artistic spirit was very much present in the ambiance and beauty of the Saint Louis World's Fair. Chicago's World's Columbia Exposition of 1903 was largely Olmsted's vision and he had direction over or a hand in the conception and construction of many of the most significant parks created in the United States. He is the father of landscape architecture. Olmsted and Calvert Vaux, who are best known as the architects of Central Park in New York City, also collaborated in the conception and construction of Prospect Park in Brooklyn. In a report to the Brooklyn park board, the two enunciated their artistic vision with ideas that echo the preceding chapter of this book:

A scene in nature is made up of various parts; each part has an individual character and its possible ideal. It is unlikely that accident should bring together the best possible ideals of each separate part, merely considering them as isolated facts, and it is still more unlikely that accident should group a number of these possible ideals in such a way that not only one or two but that all should be harmoniously related one to the other. It is evident, however, that an attempt to accomplish this artificially is not impossible.... The result would be a work of art, and the combination of the art thus defined, with the art of architecture in the production of landscape compositions, is what we denominate landscape architecture.[8]

I think it is helpful for those of us who may never have seen a pristine wilderness to contrast what it might have been through the eyes of Meriwether Lewis with those of Frederick Law Olmsted. Lewis and his companions were among the few people other than Native Americans who saw the midwestern United States before it was settled by the American East. When they entered that land it was nearly empty of human beings and teeming with animals and plants. Beautiful though it must have been, Olmsted would have been prepared to make it more beautiful by "bringing together the best possible ideals of each separate part . . . so that all should be harmoniously related to each other." A beautiful wilderness and a beautiful park have different kinds of beauty. One is the beauty of nature, the other is the beauty of art.

The wilderness entered by Lewis and Clark was made up of various parts, as is the nature of nature. The explorers delighted in finding new routes, plants, animals, vistas, peoples, and mountains. Each would, by the above observations, have its own character and possible ideal. But the relationship among these separate entities did not assure that they belonged together to form a whole that was more than the sum of its parts. The American West was also chaos in that it abounded in an incomprehensible array of new information that included riches, opportunities, and dangers. By comparison, the Saint Louis World's Fair one century later was the epitome of parts fitting together into a harmonious setting for its visitors. The experience of Lewis and Clark was much like searching the Internet as it is today. The experience of a visitor to the World's Fair was much like visiting the digital exhibit of the Haymarket described in the last chapter.

Taken as a whole, the 1904 World's Fair is, along with everything else, a supreme example of landscape architecture, a field of aesthetics and urban planning invented, along with many other things showcased in Saint Louis that year, during the 19th century. In the last chapter we looked at how entities grow from the bottom up, with parts becoming related on the basis of their meaning, and building upward to make large things or ideas. Landscape architecture is an art of working toward a beautiful whole made up of parts that are wholes in themselves with distinct character or ideals. It is gestalt thinking on a grand scale. I think that just as the 1904 World's Fair was able to showcase useful knowledge within an integrated setting, we will see the same thing developing within the Internet. Assisting toward that end is a transcending aspect of working with knowledge by selecting and combining pieces. As the architects of the 1904 World's Fair did, we need to be planning palaces and parks where different sorts of disciplines will be best accommodated and most favorably showcased. All of these could then be linked by pathways within a virtual fairground of what is known.

In the chapter about Dopey, the focus was how he could emerge as an individual creature of expression. Like a single Web page or a painting, Dopey is an artifact that is more than the sum of his parts. He is a gestalt. He also is a creature of his context: of the group of seven dwarfs, and of the movie *Snow White and the Seven Dwarfs*. Dopey also exists in other contexts, as one among his cartoon contemporaries, now senior citizens, including Mickey Mouse, Donald Duck, Bugs Bunny, and the most senior feline, Felix the Cat. Context is the arena in which single ideas form with others to cause expanded and enriched meaning. From my own watching of the migration of human knowledge into cyberspace the most profoundly fascinating aspect has been to observe and encourage the new ways in which the Internet becomes the most complete and compelling cognitive context that exists outside of the human mind.

It is instructive to compare the West that was found by Lewis and Clark with the grand exhibition that celebrated its purchase from Napoleon a century later. The first was a wilderness, like our golden swamp, and the second a world's fair of useful knowledge such as the one now forming on the Internet. There was often great beauty to be found in the wilderness. Lewis captured some of it in his writing, as in this example where he records the exquisite White Cliffs on the Missouri River in Montana:

> As we passed on it seemed as if those scenes of visionary enchantment would never have an end . . . vast ranges of walls of tolerable workmanship, so perfect indeed that I should have thought that nature had attempted here to rival the human art of masonry had I not recollected that she had first begun her work.[9]

The wilderness encountered by Lewis and Clark contained thousands of square miles that were yet virtually unaffected by human intervention. That intervention was quick to come and was underway before the expeditionary force had made it back to Saint Louis in the fall of 1806. The flood of settlement across the Mississippi into the newly opened West was fundamentally similar to the process of the cascade of knowledge (and everything else) into the Internet during the past decade. Neither was planned nor controlled very much. Both were implemented by thousands of different people and purposes, and both became churning and bubbling swamps. Both were extraordinarily productive.

The once unpopulated American West was not changed over the 19th century from the top down. Settlers trod across the new lands to homestead, prospect, set up businesses, rob banks, enforce the law, and teach. Railroad engineers blasted and leveled lines and then connected networks for the iron horse. In the 20th century, country roads were paved and then superceded by interstate highways. Thousands of people like all eight of my great-grandparents moved into the West and established residences and families. Their children sprouted and tended businesses and the professions. These and millions of other people and enterprises became interwoven into what is the chaotic civilization of the 21st century that occupies the lands first explored by Lewis and Clark. Complex adaptive systems theory is now pondered in the old western city where my Grandpa North's parents moved their young family in 1887, at the Santa Fe Institute.

The Internet has been traversed and populated much as the West was, by little pieces that grew into webs of related pages and Web sites. Digital pathways had been crossroads early on, like the old-time country intersections, but now have become elaborate interchanges like those on the interstates. Riding the roads now into and around the Internet is more information than it is possible to contemplate. That alone makes the Internet chaotic. Included in the chaos is the freshest and increasingly most cognitively compelling manifestation of humankind's useful knowledge. The current problem seems to be how to find it.

Things worked themselves out when a similar problem existed at the close of the 19th century: that century closed with showcases designed by the new aesthetic field of landscape architecture. Discovery, invention, and progress were major fruits of the 19th century. The World's Fair was an opportunity to get a direct look at the bounty, and that is what attracted the enormous crowds. There were, of course, no radio, air flight, movies, television, or Internet. Print was pretty well it for distributing knowledge, and most of that was in black and white. More than 20 million people converged on the opportunity to see the displays of useful knowledge by visiting Saint Louis for the fair.

Although there had been landscaping and parks in Europe and Asia long before the time of Frederick Law Olmsted and Central Park, Olmsted was dealt the role for landscape architecture that Lewis and Clark played for the exploration of the West. Olmsted was there first in many important ways to arrange the parts of a landscape to create a whole that was more than the sum of those parts. That required selecting, combining, and causing context. The proposal made by

Olmsted and Vaux for what became Central Park was called the Greensward Plan. The Web site of Central Park describes its ambition and challenges:

> The Greensward Plan exhibited both the sweeping meadows and lakes of the pastoral landscape and the rocky irregularity of the picturesque. The varied terrain of the land set aside for the Park invited contrasting design styles. The southern, more rolling section of the Park accommodated the tranquil, serene pastoral style. The rocky and wooded western and northern terrain inspired Olmsted and Vaux to include picturesque variation, and imperfectability in their plans.
>
> The area as a whole was a challenge to architect and engineer: rocky, swampy, and muddy. The soil was inadequate to sustain the trees and shrubs Olmsted and Vaux planned, so 500,000 cubic feet of topsoil was carted in from New Jersey. Earth was manually dug up and huge boulders blasted out. Lacking modern machinery, all materials and debris had to be carted in and out on horse-drawn carts. By 1873, more than 10 million cartloads of material had been hauled through the Park. This material included more than 4 million trees, shrubs, and plants, representing more than 1400 species that lay the foundation for what is today's Central Park. Thirty-six bridges and archways were built and four man-made water bodies, fed from the City's water supply, were created.[10]

Whether the Internet may be considered a wilderness, a swamp, or some other unplanned cyberscape, it is safe to say that it is not landscaped by design—not a park. It is, however, comparable to a chaotic city within which a park can be carved. We should be doing something like that within the Internet, especially for the useful knowledge, study disciplines, organizing truths, or whatever we want to call the important knowledge for students to learn. Or maybe it is happening spontaneously. To speculate on that is to hazard guesses, but the more I watch it the more I believe the study disciplines are following a natural process that is forming and interlinking webs of knowledge. Something just like that happened after the Cambrian Explosion, occurs within our DNA, and gives us our sight. I think the Internet has exploded into monumental size and passed the critical mass point to where it is now a primordial swamp from which a grand web of human knowledge is evolving into a world's fair of what is known to be shared in common by everyone on Earth. Such a golden fair floats above the Earth like a cloud in figure 1.1. *Cloud* is an edgy word for this because it assumes the distributed Internet is on the horizon, and that phenomenon is called the *cloud* by some who predict it. The dispersed Internet would come to reside in cyberspace itself, lifting the location of software and much more from individual servers. It is a concept that is beyond my technical grasp, but makes a wonderful misty setting for the envisioned Internet world's fair of knowledge of the future. But there is no need to wait for the cloud to form. We can and are building the intellectual Internet now. The image of the envisioned fair in figure 6.4 was made by lifting knowledge palaces from my grandparents' postcards and using some digital filters to link them and make them shine.

Along the Mississippi at the place where the Missouri comes in from the West, the change from 1804 to 1904 was from wilderness to ornate park. "Meet Me in St. Louis" once meant to get ready to go into the western wilderness, and now meant a trolley ride to a park. How modern could you get! Our ability to experience the disciplines is just as radically different today as it was even a decade ago. The changes that are here and still to come are, I think, driven by and made inevitable by the omnidimensional nature of digital media at every scale, including the macro scale which is the Internet.

Some things I have seen hint to me that an evolutionary process much like that which is attributed to physical life is already at work bringing order out of

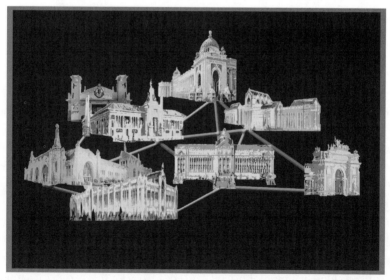

Figure 6.4. Postcards from the World's Fair were scanned, the backgrounds of the palaces dropped out, and digital filters applied to simplify and sharpen the pictures of the buildings.

chaos. A force that is understood to drive the evolution of life is the survival of the fittest—which is a process of selection. When we look at the colossal piling up of Web sites and Web pages, we could be hoping that natural selection is functioning to replicate ideas from Web pages that work and to allow those that do not to float into oblivion. Although search engines are having some luck coming up with the most frequently visited Web sites, so far we are seeing that the junk does not easily disappear. As Web pages proliferate exponentially, the few pages relevant to any one person's inquiry become a more and more minute percentage of the overall number of pages on the Internet. Because of some inherent factors within the Internet that are entirely new to organizing a communication medium, as I have said, my guess is that there will never be a means or a need to put everything in cyberspace into a neat and understandable order, nor will we have to eradicate the lousy materials or those meaningful to only a few people, like my pages are about my family's ancestors. Massive extinctions may or may not lie in the future, but we do not have to wait and see before we can form new species of Web sites.

It is a relief to realize that we may not need to clean up the mess and organize the chaos. Natural selection lifts the best out of the morass. The Google search engine process mentioned earlier does that. It records how often Web sites are visited and selects those that receive the most visits for the top of the list. It is human, cognitive choice that is making those selections because a hit is the result of a decision by someone to go to a Web page. The difficulty with the selection process in this instance is that it may not search the best Web sites for a topic. I believe more refined methods of cognitive selection are the key to creating the Internet's world fair of knowledge from the current golden swamp. An ideal form of cognitive selection has functioned for the study disciplines within the Internet since its earliest stages, and that is the listing by experts of their favorite links for their fields. Megasites for fields of study have also been around for a long time serving a function like a telephone yellow pages for listing Web sites by topic. In most specialized fields of knowledge, there are vital and often informal microwebs that relate all the best pertinent pages on the Internet to each other. The list of favorite links on the Web site of a knowledgeable specialist in a particular field is usually an ideal selection for that field. The Internet remains what it was created to be: a place of exchange among scholars.

The weblike configuration in figure 6.5 is a reflection of the structure of the universe based on the best astronomy and scientific knowledge available as I write this book. Something similar would appear from a charting of the relationships within any study discipline except those that have been artificially constructed based on a preconceived pattern like a timeline or other abstracted shape. In figure 6.5, the five largest lumps could be the main areas of a topic, such as the major languages of Europe. In that example, Latin could be at the bottom, flowing up into the Romance languages, which in turn receive Germanic and Slavic input from the right and Celtic words and patterns from the left. In a science, such as animal biology, the central mass could be one-celled animals and their descendants would flow outward into main groups and scatter further into smaller ones. As I worked with the Internet as a way to access and interface study disciplines I began to understand that the natural way to organize any set of ideas is by making their connections—and that these connections inevitably form a weblike context of facts and thoughts. On top of that, there was this wonderful aspect of the emerging structure: no matter where you entered it or where you were within it, you were always in the center of a context surrounded by related knowledge. In figure 6.5, if you are studying, say, Spanish, your context would flow out from somewhere in the middle of the web, but if you were learning Gaelic, the center of your context would be off to the left. Something else that would look like figure 6.5 would be the layout of the interior of a palace at the Saint Louis World's Fair. We know from the contemporary description cited earlier that in the Palace of Transportation:

> A huge locomotive stood in the center of the building upon a turn-table. In the western end of the building was a laboratory for testing the efficiency of locomotives. The old horse car and the modern trolley car stood side by side. The display of automobiles showed the remarkable possibilities of this new means of travel. Motor boats and other water craft were here in good numbers while the road vehicles for all sorts of purposes were not forgotten. Models of railway stations, cars and other railway equipment were displayed.[11]

If you were a visitor in the center of the grand hall, context flowed out from the huge locomotive. If the curators did their work well, one could move (perhaps it would be downward in the pattern of figure 6.5) out from the locomotive and back in time through the trolleys to the horse cars, each of which would become the center of your context as you stood, learned about it, and let your mind move back and forth in time to ponder progress. The experience of visiting knowledge interfaced on the Internet should be, and I believe inevitably will be-

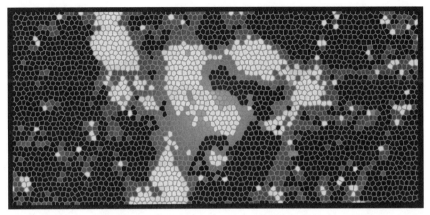

Figure 6.5. A visualization of Web site units in context, based on the structure of the known universe. Digital study discipline context can and should look like this.

come, like moving through a fair of knowledge landscaped for related meaning and thereby exhibited in context. If this strikes you as theoretical, once again I recommend to you the Rosetta Stone exhibit at the British Museum, and other examples of context travel at EdClicks.com in the Knowledge Fair pages.

The word *context* derives from the Latin word *contextus,* meaning connections, from the past participle *contexere,* meaning to weave. The connecting of Web sites weaves webs and causes context. I think the process is at best superficial if the attempt is made to create context from the top down—and that a fundamental, practical, major problem in finding and using knowledge on the Internet is that most of the resources are just lists of links that start from the top down. Take a hypothetical megasite about earth sciences. The top page might have some major entry points such as geology, meteorology, oceanography, and ecology. Clicking on each of these might lead to a page divided again into a handful of divisions of each branch of that page's sub-science. By drilling down another time or two an offering at the sixth level of geology would be something like ten links to information on volcanoes. That page would be a dead end except for volcanoes. There might be an outstanding link somewhere in meteorology including information about how weather is affected by volcanoes, but unless someone had thought to put it both in volcanoes and weather, there would be no way to move in context from where it appeared in each of the two highly separated pages. The structure of this megasite—and far too many Web sites interfacing knowledge—is like a tree, branching out to smaller and smaller units between which there is no connection without retracing steps back to where their root ideas branched.

It is quite a different experience to explore a group of Web sites that have been woven into a Weblet of context. Each single Web page becomes the center of your search while you are visiting that page. A Web page about a volcano in the South Pacific would be linked to pages of other geographically nearby volcanoes, causing paths to pages around the world with characteristics similar to the particular volcano, to pages about the composition of lava, and to pages about El Niño. By moving along these links based on context, a move is made to a new center of context, each linked to further knowledge. The links in the Knowledge Fair section at EdClicks.com will lead you into Weblets of contextual knowledge.

Being creatures of the 21st century, we no longer are bothered by, and rarely notice, Internet listings that are not in alphabetical order. That is not a necessary inconvenience in the Web environment. Along the left side of the *New York Times* online, which I have read every morning for several years, there is a vertical column of titles of sections. It has been fun to watch its order change. Only a few bits of it are in alphabetical order anymore. Even for something that is just a written list, wise displayers of visual data know that the mind that is seeking meaning prefers the most relevant stuff to be the handiest, which in the case of the *Times'* list is toward the top of the stack of words. At least this provides a suggestion of context, which does not exist at all in an alphabetical listing.

The wondrous method of growing from the bottom up to connect digital links makes it possible to be guided by laws or directions of meaning. When we look at the resulting structure from the top down we see a cosmic web. There is no real linear world except that time is linear. The cosmic web of the Universe is omnidimensional and shaped by the force of gravity. How do we shape the web of the knowledge context—or any idea—within the Web of the Internet? The Internet Web, within which a web of ideas can exist, is shaped by locations of communications transmitters and receivers. What shapes the knowledge formed within that communications web? We do. As landscape architecture shapes nature, we connect the meaning of knowledge Web sites in context. The force that causes the shape is cognitive, it is meaning. By selecting links that provide useful knowledge and then combining them by their meaning from the bottom up, we build a world's fair with palaces for the liberal arts, the sciences, and other study disciplines, and in the process pave the cognitive walkways between them.

There is a profound mystery as to why parts become wholes that end up becoming parts of other wholes until a living being is formed, and then by the same process builds up a whole sequence. Perhaps what it means to be you or means to be me arises with that process. But I find nothing within the process that tells me so. Rather, an adaptive radiation responds to a new opportunity. Where the opportunity comes from for you and me to arise is, I suppose, a theological matter. It is not as complicated with Internet knowledge content. As knowledge has combined within the Internet, we have seen that process building from the bottom up, by assembling small parts into larger ones that take on meaning, and then combine to take on a greater meaning, and so on to ever-larger combinations. The same method is effective for constructing Web pages and Web sites that provide rich cognitive materials for study.

The most compelling parallel to the formation of context as study knowledge has been placed into digital media, and the Internet is the experience we have as human beings of acquiring and relating knowledge. What the upper right portion of figure 1.1 proposes as interconnected palaces can be thought of as a mirror for the higher function of the human brain. The purpose for creating the Internet's world's fair of knowledge is to make what those online palaces contain available for the education of us all—so we can construct the fair and its palaces within the cortex of our brains.

The Internet became a golden swamp spontaneously and serendipitously. The improvement of digital expression, like the invention of cartoon animation, is going to take hard work and high artistic standards. It can lead to far more effective nuggets of knowledge for study than have ever existed. Experts in every field of knowledge should meet the challenge of creating digital knowledge nuggets that express what they know, and of making these nuggets available by tossing them now into the golden swamp.

The final phase in bringing the world's fair of knowledge into being is to select the best of the nuggets, to combine them by cognitive linking, and to do the linking sufficiently to allow context to emerge. Two factors introduced by the Internet that are completely new make success in this endeavor possible, and probably inevitable. The first is that the scale is singular, which allows one knowledge nugget to be used by all and to be kept current by one. This factor makes the fair, to put it bluntly, cheap—almost free. (There is no cost to you when you visit the Rosetta Stone page at the British Museum, and the page itself could have cost only a few pounds to create and costs almost nothing to maintain.) The second is that be-

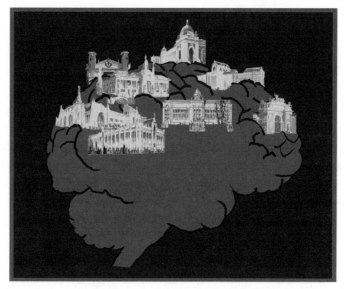

Figure 6.6.   A knowledge fair and its palaces grace the cortex of a brain.

cause the knowledge nugget is virtual, having no physical existence, it can appear redundantly in limitless places—which is not possible for hardcopy books, printed pictures, and so on. This means that not only can one nugget be used by all, but that same nugget also can appear virtually in unlimited locations and contexts. Every student can go to one nugget, one nugget can turn up in limitless topics.

The manifest destiny that compels us to organize knowledge in these new ways casts illuminating doubt on relativism. Is knowledge just what you think for you and something else that I think for me, or is it something objective outside of both of us? If we place it on a Web page, it becomes judged by those who would (or would not) connect to it. In discussing Google's search method, I defined the rating of the links there as cognitive because they are chosen by Internet surfers in general. Rich Weblets formed by subject experts are cognitively more valuable because the connections were made by the judgment of an expert. Corralling cognitive choice to make selections is key to forming the Internet fair of knowledge. The process brings us face-to-face with defining knowledge in a situation something like the one in which the Ancient Greeks found themselves. Their fundamental engagement with knowledge is described by University of North Carolina at Chapel Hill's Paddison Professor of Classics George A. Kennedy:

A unique contribution of the Greeks . . . was their interest in describing [the phenomenon of rhetoric], dividing it into categories, and giving names to the various
techniques observed so that they could be taught by others. This conceptualization of rhetoric is parallel to the conceptualization of philosophy, political theory,
grammar, and other subjects in Greece. That the Greeks could do this resulted in
a large part from the nature of the Greek language, which has a capability of coin-
ing abstract terms not found in most other languages. That the Greeks needed to
conceptualize these disciplines resulted in large part from the development, also
unique to Greece, of constitutional government. In the orderly administration of
policy making and adjudication, an individual could hope to influence decision
making by appeal to reason.[12]

Instead of conceptualizing disciplines in abstract words, today's cognitive
crowd is doing so in Web sites. The result is categorization that weaves in a context structured by reason. In chapter 5, I quoted Stephen Jay Gould's description of the emergence of life from the primordial swamp: "The history of life is
a story of massive removal followed by differentiation within a few surviving
stocks, not the conventional tale of steadily increasing excellence, complexity,
and diversity."[13] For the Internet fair of knowledge to grow, selection of the best
knowledge nuggets will be made, and that will be done by both the use of surfers
in general early on, and the choice for experts who form specialized Weblets by
linking to Web sites they have chosen. Once selected—that is, removed from the
massive Internet swamp—those Web sites and Weblets themselves will differen-
tiate and combine into cognitive context. They will link to each other based on
the meaning of the knowledge they contain. That is the process of the final two
guidelines of the six I set out in the last chapter: The fifth guideline is to allow
and encourage the natural formation of context. Because of the rich interlinking
on the Internet, context will create itself if you give it half a chance. The sixth
guideline is to pay attention to the harmony and value of the cyberscape. We
need to move beyond constructing portals and gateways. We should begin creating pavilions, parks, and fairs where exhibits are planned among well laid pathways.

One of the fascinations of this process is that it runs counter to the developed
instincts of the education establishment that has spent the past century pulling
knowledge apart and placing the bits into curricula and textbooks. Such was a
necessary evil in the need to distribute knowledge resources to thousands of
places and millions of students. Now the challenge is to let the opposite occur,

so that millions of students enter a virtual, digital web of knowledge that unites nuggets of knowledge into context. The new singularity of scale inherent in the Internet has pivoted the process full circle.

I believe the way to move into the future is not to burn all the hardcopy textbooks or to shred the 20th-century lesson plans and curricula. Those things will fade or morph into digital avatars in due course. Instead, those who are learning and teaching should be selecting knowledge nuggets from what is out there and combining them in context. Every student of any age, every teacher of a subject, and anyone who is intellectually active these days, should have a pet set of bookmarked Web sites. Scholars rely heavily on this process now. A friend of mine told me that her brother, who is in medical school, was instructed by his professors to do his research only on the Internet. Another friend, who has been an architect for 40 years, recently asked a law firm client where they wanted to put the library in their new office suite he was designing; the law partners told him not to waste floor space on a library because all of their research was done on CDs or online.

Having your own bookmarks is taking the first step: selection. The next is to combine. Underlying the new field of authoring Web sites lies a challenge like the one in figure 6.7. To get an idea how rich the digital organization can be, compare the lack of a center and failure to suggest cognitive relationships in the lists at left, which contain the same six words as those in the six boxes, with the manner in which the links among the boxes create a web of cognitive relationship. Among the six boxes, if the Weather page is your center, you have three ways to move out to related ideas; if Volcanoes is your center, you have five ways. In the alphabetical list there are no relationships suggested at all, except that the six words have some reason to be in the same list. The second list of words provides a hierarchy where it is clear only which topics are subtopics of other words. Tsunami is relegated to the study of weather, but you would miss its relationship to volcanoes by learning the list.

Here are some suggestions for how you might go about making links among your own bookmarks. You will, of course, have to begin by selecting links concerning a subject that contains knowledge that can meaningfully relate the pages to each other as earth science does in figure 6.7.

Relate each piece to every other piece in every valid relationship you can think of. The relationships you identify then become a significant part of the substance of the content of the whole Weblet, along with the pieces.

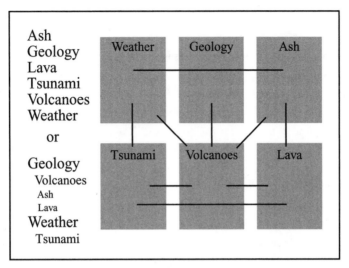

Figure 6.7. The lists at left are sorted alphabetically and by subcategory. The lines suggest links between the subjects that would be made from Web pages.

Note that patterns begin to emerge according to the structure of what they express; for example, history along a timeline and/or over a geographical area.

Enter at any point to relish a piece and to move from it in any direction in context. Content creates context because it builds from the inside out.

Notice that gestalts, defined as the wholes being more than the sum of its parts, will arise spontaneously—although your ability to link the parts is key. You might, for example, in working with figure 6.7, link up a combination of the pages that would be a Weblet for weather related to volcanoes. That would be a new topic not suggested by any single link, but arising as a pattern of their relationships.

Gestalts, in turn, should be identified as pieces and linked to related gestalts. Content is building up from underneath and thus context emerges like life itself.

This process scales from the relationships on a Web page—among text boxes, images, links, and other content—to the relationships among pages on a Web site, to the relationships among Web sites on the Internet.

Far from being contrived, the process we have been looking at is intuitive and natural. It is alphabetical order that is a simplistic abstraction nearly devoid of cognitive suggestion. In human thinking it almost impossible to avoid context. When an idea pops up it is within an environment of related thought, and it is very easy to move in our minds from this idea to that one. When we are not given ideas in a setting, we supply them. Shakespeare knew that and performed his plays on a stage essentially without sets. The dialog sets the stage with phrases like "fair yonder moon," which when intoned by the actor caused the moon to be virtually hung in the sky for the audience. Bookmarking and listing favorite links has been a spontaneous reaction from the first days of the Internet. People jumped at the opportunity to combine into context what was available. The response was inherent in how people think. Still, the result of bookmarking is more like a swamp than a fair.

The Internet golden swamp is a new continent of wilderness that has been flooded with settlement and now beckons landscaping and construction. Like towns, cities, roads, and highways, what is built must be useful. The question before us, in this era when the rush into the Internet with the substance of study disciplines is becoming complete and the swamp the Internet has become is increasingly challenging to plumb, is if and how rise will be given to a great digital world's fair of knowledge. In the last chapter I urged the invention of new forms of digital expression, and that experts in fields of knowledge use Web sites and expressive tools to place tutorials for what they know into the golden swamp. I conclude this chapter with a challenge to build exhibit halls and palaces. For this to be done well, I believe progress needs to be made in two areas. First, there should be development of formats and templates for maximizing the connectivity potential of Web pages and squelching the urge to make lists. Second, as we move beyond the simple mark-up language of HTML into more powerful ways to identify and relate Web sites, the palaces and fair will be easier to effect, and we must take advantage of the new methods.

In the meantime, we should continue the transformation of Internet research and scholarship from text-searching to palace-building. The British Museum has served as an example of experts who are weaving Weblets of their expertise into exhibit halls for virtual palaces of history and archaeology. The American Institute of Physics hosts an online Center for the History of Physics[14] that offers outstanding exhibits on Madam Curie, Albert Einstein, the Discovery of the Electron, and other topics, along with carefully chosen links to other physics Web pages. Beyond the two just mentioned, there are thousands of other examples of excellent knowledge nuggets which offer links to related nuggets selected by the experts who reach out from their own pages to link to others that they respect. The expertorial movement on the Internet has two parts. The first is to hope that experts in myriad fields will create their own exhibits that, like Dopey, are expressive, becoming digital tutors from which the knowledge of their host experts can be learned by others online. The second is for the experts who create tutorials to select superior related knowledge nuggets and to link out from their expertorials to these Web sites, forming a Weblet that acts as an expert exhibit for their field of expertise.

Then who is to build the grand palaces and the park? Who will have the vision to see into the future, as did Frederick Law Olmsted? Witold Rybczynski's fine book about Olmsted is titled *A Clearing in the Distance.* The title is a tribute to the remarkable ability that Olmsted had, and which a landscape architect must cultivate, to plan and plant to achieve a result in the future. Not only must the architect see the gold in the swamp, but must envision as well the fair completed and in full swing. Fortunately these days there is "Internet time" and things happen a lot faster than trees grow in parks.

The Saint Louis World's Fair was a masterful combination of fun, elegance, and a theme that made all the exhibitors want to come to show off what they had. The landscape and building architects designed the setting, but it was actually a matrix formed to interface what was contained therein: people coming to look at knowledge and the knowledge they came to look at. The inherent relationships of the knowledge itself guided the planning: history went into the Liberal Arts Palace, the locomotives and automobiles went into the Transportation Palace, corn went into the Iowa Pavilion, and the Buddhas went into the Ceylon Pavilion. The buildings were arranged among pathways for the easy movement of people among palaces and lovely vistas, causing the formation of an overall plan, and the fair itself arose as a grand gestalt.

The parallel of the grand event to a virtual fair of knowledge on the Internet is appropriate. Perhaps we shall have that fair by 2004, and that would be very fine. The virtual one would be knowledge imbedded in a matrix of context formed by the cognitive relationships of the nuggets of knowledge. Pathways would allow movement through the fair by those who came to see the knowledge. Much of this structure already exists and is heavily trafficked within the golden swamp that is today's Internet. Perhaps it will not be lifted out as I have suggested in figure 1.1, but that would be a wonderful thing to do. It would require the inspiration and effort of something comparable to the backers of the Saint Louis World's Fair or the park boards of New York and Brooklyn that promoted Central Park and Prospect Park, and followed through to get them built. It would take thinking like Olmsted's to oversee the connections of things. It would include the showcasing of what is known by experts from every field of useful knowledge. The Massachusetts Institute of Technology (MIT) has caught the spirit and is in the process of posting materials containing knowledge for the courses it offers online, including lecture notes, problem sets, syllabuses, simulations, and video lectures. Thinking of the process as building a grand structure, MIT computer science and engineering Professor Hal Abelson, comparing the knowledge-offering principle to the open source software movement: "Fundamentally, they proceed from the same ethic, which has to do with sharing. In the Middle Ages people built cathedrals, where the whole town would get together and make a thing that's greater than any individual person could do and the society would kind of revel in that. We don't do that as much anymore, but in a sense this is kind of like building a cathedral."[15]

I hope it happens soon. It would be quite easy to do because it would require no land or buildings and a great many of the exhibits themselves already exist, though they will become more handsome and instructive as they grow more expressive in the future. You may be thinking that lots of lists of links exist on the Internet already, but they are not a fair of knowledge. They tend to block progress somewhat by the frustration they create because they are not connected in context and they flow from the top down into dead ends. Context is minimal and that tends to cause them to become cognitively vapid. The fair will be a web, and I believe moving beyond HTML and into more powerful languages will provide new tools for combining digital assets. A quarter of a million links would probably be enough, each one being selected as the best on the Internet for its particular nugget of knowledge and linked out to superb links related to the knowledge it contained at a lower level of detail than its own. The quarter million links that compose the fair would all have one or more links to each other. Every link would appear in as many combinations as the relationships that are assigned to it. Context would be flexible and rich. I think that the fair is developing right now, though we remain as unexpectant as were the people described by Henry Adams who were surprised by the explosion of change that characterized the 19th century. The new world's fair of useful knowledge will be a beautiful thing when it happens, and it will be the common destination of everyone who seeks to learn. In the meantime we already enjoy a golden swamp, within which abounds global common knowledge that is liberating the defining gift of teaching.

NOTES

1. Stephen E. Ambrose, *Undaunted Courage* (New York: Simon & Schuster, 1996), 52–53.

2. *American Philosophical Society,* "About the APS," www.amphilsoc.org/about/ [accessed 15 August 2001].

3. *American Institute of Physics,* "The Quantum and the Cosmos I," www.aip.org/ history/einstein/quantum1.htm [accessed 15 August 2001].

4. *American Institute of Physics,* "The Quantum and the Cosmos I."

5. Sam'l. F. Myerson, *The Greatest of Expositions: Completely Illustrated* (St. Louis, Missouri, 1904), quoted on WashingtonMo.com, "1904 World's Fair," www.washingtonmo. com/1904/p4.htm [accessed 28 May 2001].

6. *Terry's 1904 World's Fair Page,* www.inlink.com/terryl/transport.html [accessed 15 August 2001].

7. Julia E. Spaulding, diary, private collection of Stewart W. Breck.

8. Witold Rybczynski, *A Clearing in the Distance* (New York: Scribner, 1999), 274.

9. *State of Montana,* "Lewis and Clark," lewisandclark.state.mt.us/sites.idc? IDNumber=5 [accessed 2 September 2001].

10. *Central Park,* "Central Park History: 1858–1878," www.centralparknyc.org/ cp-1858–1878.html [accessed 29 August 2001].

11. *Terry's 1904 World's Fair Page.*

12. George A. Kennedy, ed., *Aristotle on Rhetoric: A Theory of Civil Discourse* (New York: Oxford University Press, 1991), 8.

13. Stephen Jay Gould, *Wonderful Life* (New York: W.W. Norton, 1989), 25.

14. *American Institute of Physics,* "Center for the Study of Physics," www.aip.org/ history/ [accessed 29 August 2001].

15. Carey Goldberg. "Auditing Classes at M.I.T., on the Web and Free," *New York Times on the Web,* www.nytimes.com/2001/04/04/technology/04MIT.html [accessed 4 April 2001].

7

HOW WE REALLY LEARN

The Gift of Teaching

On the morning of 11 September 2001, the crash of airliners into the two tallest skyscrapers on Manhattan Island occurred above a location that had been below the surface of the great river when it was discovered for Europe by Henry Hudson. A new millennium was shattered in its infancy with a terrifying reminder of the human capacity for evil. Across much of the world a clamor to eradicate terrorism was almost immediate, and a wistful sense that things would never be the same was the mood of the time. Pandora was at it again! The plot that had been unfolding for the 21st century for technical progress and global prosperity swerved and it seemed like the *deus ex machina* had suddenly released terrorism on the world stage. Things, though, were not really all that new. Terrorism slithered onto the stage of history with the first bite into the apple from the Tree of the Knowledge of Good and Evil. Terrorism is an ancient wickedness: the knowing choice of bad over good. What evil is and the behavior it engenders, such as terrorism, are not defined by religions; religions are measured by how they strive to contain the wicked part of the nature of humankind, which we can choose to let loose because we have free will. Evil lurks on the world stage as an ever-present villain.

Separate from religion, which combats evil by teaching moral choice based in faith, is another force against evil and its practitioners: truth. Truth, like evil, is not a doctrine created by a particular group of people or their theories. (You may disagree, but I am on practical, not speculative, ground here.) The truth that the American Enlightenment called useful knowledge, and that John Dewey termed the organizing bodies of truth that we call studies, can belong to everybody. Its purpose, as Benjamin Franklin put it, is to "let Light into the Nature of Things, tend to increase the Power of Man over Matter, and multiply the Conveniences or Pleasures of Life."[1] Ignorance is the absence of the kind of truth Franklin meant by useful knowledge. Ignorance creates an efficacious environment for the promotion of evil and of evil's active thrusts that we are experiencing in the 21st century as terrorism. The purpose of education is to teach the useful knowledge—the organizing bodies of truth. It is possible to lie to educated people. Adolf Hitler certainly proved that. His favorite technique was what he called the big lie because he realized the bigger the lie he told the less likely that those who heard it could accept that anyone would tell such a whopper. A friend of mine who was a U.S. soldier during the Allied occupation of Germany had learned German as a child in the Midwest. He told me he had asked many German civilians in a town near what had been a concentration camp why they did nothing, and they still were saying that the camp had just been a place where captured people were put to work. Hitler was a large and very clever liar, but his more powerful persuasions over his educated Germans were manipulation of prejudices and historical wounds. He gained control in spite of the education of his populace, not because of their ignorance. The latter method is far more common and a lot easier.

When it takes 4,000 donkeys to deliver just a few books to thousands of children, the risk of ignorance for those kids is very high. Their vulnerability should remind us that in addition to diplomatic, military, social, and religious action, there is another sort of campaign that can mitigate against terrorism and diminish legion human woes: it is the elimination of ignorance. Filling the gaping knowledge voids in the brains of billions of children has become doable for the first time ever because of the Internet. The realization forced on us by 21st-century terrorism of the need to make a better world provides new focus to push ahead against ignorance. Ignorance is no stranger to the homeland, in places like Chicago schools where half the children cannot read and half the children cannot do their math. In the context of the metaphors of this book, ignorance is a higher cortex that is pretty much empty. Its owner can barely read, or not read at all. At most it may contain a few foundations, but ignorance for our visual metaphor is the absence of palaces containing the study disciplines. The cortex of a person who is ignorant of the disciplines does not contain knowledge of history, literature, arts, mathematics, sciences, technology, and the rest of what we suppose are taught at school. Figure 7.1 depicts the opposite of ignorance: it is

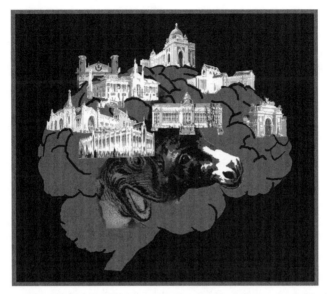

Figure 7.1. A fair of knowledge becomes a park graced by palaces erected in the higher cortex above the more primitive aspects of a brain.

a learned or educated mind. As we leave ignorance and become educated we lay foundations and build palaces and pathways among them—creating over a lifetime of learning and thought our own personal fair of knowledge set in our own parkland in which we may amble mentally and relish the beauty and fascination of what we have acquired from that which is known by humankind. With luck and effort, we may even experience creative thought by putting things together in new ways within our palaces of thought. That personal haven of knowledge and thought is also a crucial place for any person to look to evaluate his opinions and actions as a citizen of his culture, country, and world.

Each of our parks is unique. There is general similarity among all the chemists, all the medievalists, and all the geographers. Certain foundations are shared by all educated people because they are basic, observable truths, like the multiplication tables and dates in history. Communication is made possible by other foundations, like grammar and vocabulary. But the contents of no two human brains among the billions that exist can be exactly the same. There are three major reasons this is so; the first two are happy ones and the third one has caused much of the greatest trouble experienced over the ages by human beings. The first reason no two brains will contain the same knowledge is the stunning flexi-

bility and awesome potential of the organ itself. If you and I study a flower together, we will observe similar things but we will also observe different things,
and as we do our observing, we will put what we see together in different ways
and relate it to other things we know. Everything you or I ever learned or thought
contributes to the sum of what we know—which forms the palaces and pathways
of our minds. The second major reason everyone has a unique store of knowledge is the immeasurable magnitude of human knowledge. One supposes that a
family of hunter-gatherers isolated from all people except their own small tribe
might pretty well have been able to share comprehensively, and each acquire
everything known to that particular people. But even then, if a member of the
tribe discovers a new flower, she suddenly knows something unique to her.
These days the world is drowning in knowledge and specialists struggle to keep
up with even the smallest fields. Even for the hunter-gatherer, and certainly for
any person in the 21st century, learning is a matter of selecting from swamps of
knowledge, and then combining the selected bits into meaningful gestalts that
become linked among themselves by pathways of thought.

The third reason people have not been able to acquire and build similar personal internal knowledge has been the denial of equal access to knowledge; a few
could ladle deeply from all the swamps but most could dip only superficially into
some shallow puddles. A big factor throughout history has been elitism and
tyranny where enforced ignorance is used as a means of dominance and power.
Geography and economics have also been major reasons that not all children
have been exposed to and able to learn knowledge equally. Thomas Jefferson had
a plan "to diffuse knowledge more generally through the mass of people." In
1782 he described it in his *Notes on Virginia:*

> This bill proposes to lay off every county into small districts of five or six miles
> square, called hundreds, and in each of them to establish a school for teaching
> reading, writing, and arithmetic. The tutor to be supported by the hundred, and
> every person in it entitled to send their children three years gratis, and as much
> longer as they please, paying for it. These schools to be under a visitor who is an-
> nually to choose the boy of best genius in the school, of those whose parents are
> too poor to give them further education, and send him forward to one of the gram-
> mar schools, of which twenty are proposed to be erected in different parts of the
> country, for teaching Greek, Latin, Geography, and the higher branches of nu-
> merical arithmetic. Of the boys thus sent in one year, trial is to be made at the

grammar schools one or two years, and the best genius of the whole selected, and continued six years, and the residue dismissed. By this means twenty of the best geniuses will be raked from the rubbish annually, and be instructed at public expense, so far as the grammar schools go. At the end of six years' instruction, one half are to be discontinued . . . ; and the other half, who are to be chosen for the superiority of their parts and disposition, are to be sent and continued three years in the study of such sciences as they shall choose, at William and Mary College.[2]

Jefferson envisioned the schools[3] as "teaching all the children of the State reading, writing, and common arithmetic" while turning out "superior genius" from among those whose school was underwriting publicly, while "furnishing to the wealthier part of the people convenient schools at which their children may be educated at their own expense." The higher education was allotted only to the boys.

Although I believe the coming free and easy access to knowledge will undermine enforced ignorance, there is a more certain and revolutionary way that the unequal access to knowledge will end. The children in Chicago grade schools, the junior high school students from Brooklyn with whom I chatted by the Intrepid, the kids at the Eastside private school a couple of miles away where the teacher told me he had never had to teach a little boy how to use a mouse, and the youngsters in the Afghan mountains who receive books on donkey-back— each have very different knowledge exposure. These four sets of kids (and everybody else) will soon not only have access to knowledge, but they will have exactly the same access because they will be using a single source in common for most of the particular aspects of what is known. Everyone will access the same digital can or palace. That is not speculative, it is happening.

As an example, everyone will be able go to the free Web pages of knowledge being placed online by MIT. Everyone can already go to the Rosetta Stone page at the British Museum. Yes, there are the tasks of getting the machines to the students, of language translation, of locating pertinent pages, and the need for the world's young people to gain the skills to read and study on MIT's pages, and all the rest. But the fundamental obstacles of distance and distribution have crumbled. It does not take a donkey to deliver a book, with a very few scraps from rich knowledge like what an institution like MIT may teach, over a rocky pass into the inner mountain valleys of Afghanistan. The actual Web pages created and maintained at MIT can be studied virtually by any student anywhere. When a student has a foundation to lay or a palace to build she can find what she seeks to construct it in her own mind using the virtual palaces that are rising within the Internet. As MIT president Charles M. Vest speculated about the knowledge that will be made available by the vaunted academic institution he leads: "I . . . suspect in this country and throughout the world, a lot of bright, precocious high school students will find this a great playground [and ultimately] there will probably be a lot of uses that will really surprise us and that we can't really predict."[4]

By placing knowledge nuggets online and making them free we utterly eliminate entrance requirements for their study. One remaining physical step is having the machines in hand that accesses the knowledge, but when those become as easy to obtain as transistor radios, they cease to be a significant barrier. In the meantime computers connected to telephone wires are proliferating in teaching centers across the world. That leaves still one more barrier: the kid has to be able to understand what she accesses. We have now come full circle to the question of other people's children. Is there something inherent in the individual child that qualifies her to feed at the trough of human knowledge? If so, is it gender, race, sufficient leisure to allow for study, class, religion, intelligence, or some combination of the foregoing? In the past, all of these and still other factors have been deemed appropriate filters for sifting kids to decide which ones to allow access to knowledge.

Figure 7.2 is something Thomas Jefferson could not have imagined. World sophisticate that he was, he knew that only a very few individuals, and almost no women, could expect to visit the great hallowed halls of central libraries, museums, and colleges where significant repositories of knowledge could be accessed. His enlightened and democratic spirit designed a system by which selected geniuses could be moved up from the masses and be given access to higher learning. Today, everyone can have that access, and that is an astounding change. Horace Mann would have loved it. Lawrence A. Cremin described Mann's passion and vision in his essay *Horace Mann's Legacy:* "Mann's school was to be common, not in the traditional European sense of a school for the common people, but in a new sense of a school common to all people. It was to be available and equal to all, part of the birthright of every American child."[5] In the same paragraph a later sentence explains another purpose that motivated Horace Mann's dream and that does not exist with the Internet common school: " [Mann's common school] would mix the children of all creeds, classes, and backgrounds, the warm association of childhood kindling a spirit of mutual

Figure 7.2.   Physically speaking, the need for more than one knowledge location no longer exists. Should everyone use knowledge in common?

amity and respect which the strains and cleavages of adult life could never destroy."[6] Using the Internet in common soon will be students in mansions and ghettos, igloos and tents, jungles and deserts. They will wear blazers or t-shirts, miniskirts or hijab, uniforms or gang garb. The theorems of geometry, the process of mitosis, the elevation of mountains, and the unfolding insights into genomics are the same for all. When you think about it, the paradigm shift is glorious: instead of unalike children mixed together physically (and there is nothing wrong with that, except it has nothing whatsoever to do with the study disciplines like math and grammar) the children share equally the totally neutral arena of truth. We can and should continue to assure the warm association of childhood in the nurturing of each person. This goal should be a major consideration in envisioning and designing the environments into which we place our little ones as they are growing up. The Dutch managed to do that by sending them all outside to play so they would not mess up their orderly houses. The mingling is marvelous, but it is not the teaching of useful knowledge.

There is, however, a mingling of minds that establishes another sort of rapport and that is the collegiality sparked by common knowledge. I recall in the spring of 1961 when the debate teams I had been coaching were to compete in the West Texas regionals, the El Paso school district provided a large bus to transport the city winners in all of the Interscholastic categories to Odessa, Texas, where the next round of competition was held. The trip is about 300 miles, requiring that the students and chaperons spend several hours on the bus each way. Although school spirit was strong and the kids were from several different high schools that consistently competed against each other in sports and academic events, school identity quickly melted as the kids bonded by their skills. I have a distinct memory of the math competitors from three schools in league with each other as they were cheating discus-throwers and weightlifters at cards. (We broke that up.) I am confident that if a superior math student from Dallas or Timbuktu had been on the bus, she would soon have been conspiring with the other sharks to fool the jocks at cards. The forensics competitors also bonded, spending all three days together, and the theater competitors became a clique. What surfaced with those adolescents becomes magnetic in academic fields, research, and intellectual and professional specialties. Those who conduct active intellectual lives are aware of their peers and relish exchanges with them. What is as thick as a nest of linguists, or herpetologists, or classicists? Competitive at times for sure, but the enjoyment of peers is the shared knowledge and the common curiosity about the same knowledge.

It is breathtaking to realize that the objects of the animated curiosity of the linguists, herpetologists, classicists—and every other area of study—is now shared by them online and potentially by any of the students in the groups named by Thomas Jefferson: from the children just undertaking to read and write to the geniuses engaged at the highest level of education. Examples of places they or you can peer over the shoulders of knowledge experts are at EdClicks.com in the Common Knowledge section. The Internet provides a common knowledge into which every child, every scholar, and anyone else dropping by may dip. This common knowledge is universal and unrestricted, and is transforming education as we have known it. Like the golden swamp of Amsterdam, it raises a mist that stimulates thinking and originality. Unattached from school buildings, the common knowledge admits everyone, without regard to age, sex, race, tribe, nation, or persuasion. Young and old may dip into it and learn, at their individual pace and preference. The great and growing common fair of knowledge provides increasing links from learners to the learned, and ways are being refined to enhance the personal interplay. This common knowledge is already one of the great achievements of our species, and it is not even very sophisticated yet. In a time when religious, tribal, and cultural sensitivities can seem intractable, cyberspace is the domain of the individual. Though it may still seem like a swamp, it is actually the great ocean of human knowledge now brimming with opportunity and adventure. A kid caught in a dismal family, neighborhood, or school, an African savanna or Asian mountain valley, can jump into a silicon chip to go out to the ocean, and find a far horizon. We are all that kid, in one way or another. The cascade of knowledge into the Internet is washing over the world and giving each of us the captaincy of our own mind.

Actually, the captaincy of one's own mind is a fundamental urge and expectation for any human being. Ignorance is not our natural state. Curiosity is almost as powerful a drive in children as hunger, perhaps more powerful. Tyranny has to work hard at preserving an individual's ignorance. Kids are sponges. When book learning is available they soak it up, and in any event they absorb the traditions of their culture and learn about the things that surround them in their environments. You can be sure the kids in the Afghan mountains know a very great deal about donkeys and their rugged home terrain. Ignorance is forced on human nature and the resistance to it of the young individual is strong, at least for the early years, although minds can indeed be dulled by intellectual boredom, and misinformation can produce fanatics. Putting it positively: If the knowledge is there, young people are inclined to take it in, and the good news is that knowledge is more available to more young people than ever before—and soon to virtually all of them.

The little girl in figure 7.2 is dressed as my great-grandmother Lizzy would have been at her age. The other person in the figure is meant to suggest any of several kinds of people: a college or graduate student or professor, a scholar from a strange foreign location (the garb is labeled Norwegian on the 19th-century advertising card from which I scanned it), an inquiring adult not related to education, or a teacher. Both figures lead to some thoughts about how we will learn in the 21st century.

The fact that the little girl is dipping into knowledge in common with advanced scholars would have seemed shocking to many people of her time, except of course for Mary Lyon. Mary would have heartily approved. Another question that rocks the foundation of some education theories: is she too young to be doing that? There is the rub! It seems especially unlikely that other people's children could do it when they are that young. She will probably become frustrated no matter who she is, and her development may be stunted. It is too hard for her. It is too soon. If these objections are valid it means one of two things: either children should wait to a certain older age before they are taught very much, or they should be offered watered-down versions of the disciplines with the expectation that when they are older they will get the full knowledge. I am quick to point out that the latter, easier stuff can be included on the Internet, and indeed is there, usually in a Web site marked for education instead of for a knowledge subject. When you find chemistry on an education site it may have little animals acting out the parts of elements. When you find it on a working laboratory's Web site the animals are gone and the elements are presented in a straightforward manner.

I once watched the video of a focus group where boys in their early teens were being asked for their opinions about various knowledge resources on the Internet. The theme of the questioning had to do with which Web sites they would use to do their homework. After about a half hour of politely (they were getting paid) commenting on different Web sites, one of the guys was shown a very extensive database where grade level was absent and there were hundreds of physics links to laboratories, animations, and college lecture notes. He already had responded to several earlier questions about his homework methods, but brightened up when he was asked when he would use such an extensive database. He said, "Oh, I would go there if I really wanted to find out something." His spontaneous words made it clear that he did not think of homework and finding out something as the same thing. I believe he relished the latter because he was the captain of his mind. If he felt that way and managed his acquisition of knowledge that way, why have the homework, and why have a teacher? You may have wondered why no school or teacher can be seen in the picture of 21st century education used in this book and at the EdClicks.com Web site. The reasons for those two missing elements are very different, the one being absence and the other being presence.

No school is depicted because schools may well disappear, at least as we knew them in the 20th century. Currently they barely exist in many parts of the world. If a planner today were to envision schooling anew for an area where it does not exist, he would be unlikely to take the approach Thomas Jefferson did. He would be more likely to do something like phone companies tend to do now in under-developed areas: rely on wireless. I do not know whether my grandnephew Kyle, born in 2001, will sit in rows in classes in a building designated as a school by the time he is in junior high. I would bet a great deal that his knowledge resource will be the Internet with which he will interact wirelessly. Perhaps he will be apprenticed at nine, as Michelangelo was, to an art or work in a studio as Rembrandt did in his teens. If he has a bent to the sciences, he may be following the progress of research at a biotech lab or a great telescope in Hawaii—not in Hawaii, of course, but virtually, through the Internet. I feel pretty sure he will be well limbered up intellectually by Socratic challenges as his teachers exhort explanation and support for the knowledge he prizes. I would bet my bonnet he will be active in one or more forms of articulation—in writing composition, in the visual or performing arts, or in my favorite, debate. I doubt that what are considered schools will be thought of as buildings because since knowledge is no longer pinned down to a place, and all of it can be carried in a pocket, the events of childhood and youth will be portable too.

Can other people's children handle a life like that? We must be willing to face up to questioning the necessity and wisdom of sentencing children to 12 years in physical schools. The justification that it is necessary for them to be so confined in order for them to obtain knowledge is evaporating. It is doing them a profound disservice to make them stay in 20th-century-like schools because we have not figured out what else to do with them all day. Maybe the Dutch had the right idea. In Lincoln's day and just about always before that there was plenty of work that children could do and were expected to do. Maybe we have to keep them together in institutions for socialization, and because they must be trained to manage the other parts of the brain, as the image with the donkey and the reptile suggest. If that is the case, the incarceration is not about knowledge, it is an institutional substitute for parenting and for the roles once played by culture and religion. I hope there is a better solution. There is work to be done before we can know how long institutions we now call schools might endure and what the experience of children might morph into in the future.

Teachers, on the other hand, are here to stay—in fact, they are back! They have always been absolutely necessary and play a crucial role in shaping the future of each of us and all of us. No teacher is depicted in figure 1.1, of how we will learn in the 21st century, because the teacher's relationship to the image is that of a painter to the canvas. For too long, a teacher has been viewed as a cog on a wheel of education. That is getting things backward, because education is the product of teaching. That another person learn is the goal and work of a teacher. In our figure, it is an act of teaching to pour knowledge into the Internet; to organize it into meaningful units within the swamp; to elevate these units into a digital matrix and there to link them into palaces of context and to pave pathways among these; and, to instruct a student in the use of a wireless access device for knowledge. When any person performs one of these tasks, he or she is then being a teacher. All of us are teachers at times. Parents are teachers a lot of the time. A herpetologist is a teacher when he puts an animation of a frog online from which frog knowledge jumps out at a person visiting his Web page. A wireless wonk is being a teacher when she programs a circuit that facilitates the interface of cognitive connections.

Here are some things teaching is not: taking attendance, grading multiple-choice test papers (as compared with grading and commenting on essays), handing out demerits, chaperoning the prom, or counseling a battered child. Guts and gifts are required to do all of those jobs well. Teaching, though, is something different. To teach is to show a person something; *show* is the oldest root meaning of the word *teach*. To use a fancier word, teaching is *pedagogy*, literally leading or escorting someone to knowledge. In figure 1.1 the young person (or it could be any person) tapping into and learning knowledge without the participation of a teacher brings into focus a key muddle of 20th-century education. Just where is the teacher in this picture? Certainly some mechaphobia is caused by fearing that the teacher is no longer needed. The answer is that if the person with the wireless device is absorbing useful knowledge, the teacher's task for that endeavor by the student has been successfully completed for she has led him to the knowledge; she cannot learn it for him. In another setting, the teacher can assume a Socratic role with the student by challenging him to articulate what he has learned and to defend it using other knowledge from his store. It is certainly not my intent to downgrade the teacher as a questioner and guide, but it is a muddle indeed when we expect our teachers to be the source of knowledge. Just as Lincoln was in his childhood, I would be impressed by such a straggler wizard. Certainly teachers should have their own intellectual palaces, but these need not be depended on as the source for what their students learn, and most certainly should not remain that source over time for young people if they are to become educated.

Looking back once again at our little girl in figure 7.2 and the young boy in figure 1.1, we see children who apparently can read, work with numbers, and use a digital machine. We know that today's kids have no difficulty acquiring the last of those skills, and seem to be mysteriously born knowing how to use a mouse and immune to mechaphobia. That leaves what Jefferson called "reading, writing, and arithmetic" and Lincoln called "readin, writin, and cypherin." My thesis has been that this sequence of developments is under way: what is known by humankind is nearing completion of its cascade into the Internet golden swamp; artistic innovation is overdue and should be soon coming, therefore making digital interfacing of knowledge cognitively compelling in potent new ways; and, as topics congeal into an outstanding few Web sites for each kernel of knowledge these will be interlinked by pathways of meaning to form a great new world's fair of useful knowledge accessible to all. What is left, then, is to make certain all children receive the minimum that young Virginians were to have, what the Dutch children managed to get from their chaotic schools, and what the young Lincoln acquired before he set out on his courses of self-tutelage. Rather than trying to argue here that doing so will be sufficient to let youngsters begin building their own foundations of knowledge by using the Internet, I refer you to the section on EdClicks.com called the Ladder of Knowledge. You will find examples there of places to learn simple things and to learn things simply.

Providing the "readin, writin, and cypherin" is the final ingredient that completes the definition of teaching, which is "to show," and to lead children to knowledge. The first role teachers of the 21st-century play for students is to show them how to read, write, and use numbers to interface with the common knowledge on the Internet. It does not matter whether that teaching is done with chalkboard or paper and pencil, carved on mud tablets, drawn in the sand—or clicked online. Citizens of Earth who do not have these skills are denied our common knowledge; those who do have them now have the opportunity to attain an equality never before imaginable. The second step is to show students how to use the common knowledge—to lead them to it. The fellow in the focus group was eager to do that: to find out something.

The quest for knowledge is both a lonely individual endeavor and a means of exciting engagement with fellow beings. If you have ever taught a class, you know that knowledge is not learned by classes, but by individual students. You can almost see a light switch on for a kid in the fourth row, and then another kid over by the window. I used to teach the young teenagers when they took a communicant class before they became full members of the Fifth Avenue Presbyterian Church in New York City. I remember trying to think of a way to explain the relationship of the New Testament to the Old Testament in the Bible. Early on the Sunday morning when I was to teach that lesson I noticed a little frosted glass jar with a short, fat candle inside. It was a gift to me from a young nephew and it was not a religious symbol but in fact had a cute image of a mouse painted on it. But it was perfect for the lesson when the idea for using it popped into my mind. When we got to the point I had to make in class, I set the candle on the table and announced that it was the Old Testament. I explained that its glass had some semi-ornate curves and edges which represented history, teachings, and tradition developed over many centuries. I then gave a book of matches to one of the students and asked him to light the candle. He had to pick it up and turn it sideways, sticking the match inside where the wick stuck up about halfway toward the top of the glass opening. When it was lit the candle inside the frosted exterior caused the little jar to glow. I said that the New Testament was the flame and the relationship of the New Testament to the Old Testament was the same as that of the flame to the candle and glowing jar. We talked about how the flame was why the little jar had been created and that it fulfilled the jar's purpose. Some related ideas arose and the articulation was interesting. The only problem we had was, when class was over, none of us wanted to blow the candle out.

This little lesson is online at EdClicks.com. What I did or said in class and what I put online have no effect on the actual relationship between the two testaments; that exists outside and independent of me and has done so for millennia. The animation can convey that relationship to individuals I will never see or know. Each of my students and each person who may grasp the idea of the relationship online will do that as a single individual. Knowledge has an objective existence, and what we take in as our knowledge we do as individuals. I was being a teacher when I showed the candle to the kids: I showed them the knowledge. I was a teacher when I put the animation online for the same reason. Of course I treasure the experience of the articulation with the kids, and that is teaching too. The fact that I could convey the idea to someone I will never know does not make me less of a teacher.

Knowledge is never a gift created by the teacher. The teacher guides a student to it or holds up a sign or a token of it. (*Token* is another root word for *teach*.) The candle, or its image as an online animation, is a token of the relationship between the testaments. The token, and the knowledge itself, must be grasped by the student and no one can do it for her. I think that the new era of common knowledge gives new urgency and efficacy to what Kant wrote of as self-tutelage and defined as enlightenment. The greatest and most liberating gift of teaching is to show someone how to acquire knowledge on their own. The future offers virtually limitless opportunity to guide individuals to knowledge that is unknown to billions of people now. The gifts that teaching bestows on students are essentially the skills of reading, of writing, of arithmetic, and, from that platform, the gift of pointing the way to knowledge. Socratic questioning and the coaching of articulation activities are ways of doing the latter, of pointing the way to knowledge. Indeed, informed discourse is a sublime pleasure of being human.

Ultimately your enthusiasm and mine for how we will learn in the 21st century as I have described it comes down to our respective faith in other people's children to captain their own minds in their quest for useful knowledge. At its purest, teaching is an act of liberation: the gift to another mind of letting go. Meriwether Lewis had a pinnacle experience with that gift when he left the White House after spending two years with President Jefferson, who had performed as a quintessential teacher. What Jefferson gave Lewis was not knowledge; rather he pointed his pupil to knowledge. He did not tell his student what he would find. Instead he taught him what to look for and how to do it, and then sent him into a vast unexplored land to learn and record on his own. Jefferson anticipated eagerly what knowledge the returning Lewis would show to him! To point to and guide students into useful knowledge is not a new definition of *teaching;* it is the oldest meaning of the word. The fact that all the children of all other people on our planet can receive the gift of teaching by letting them go as captains of their own minds into the common knowledge of humankind is completely new. When we make and let that happen, our planet will put a final end to ignorance.

NOTES

1. *American Philosophical Society*, "About the APS," www.amphilsoc.org/about/ [accessed 15 August 2001].

2. Thomas Jefferson, *Notes on Virginia, 1782–83*, "The Life and Selected Writings of Thomas Jefferson" (New York: The Modern Library, Random House, 1944), 262–63.

3. Jefferson, *Notes on Virginia*, 263.

4. Carey Goldberg. "Auditing Classes at M.I.T., on the Web and Free," *New York Times on the Web*, www.nytimes.com/2001/04/04/technology/04MIT.html [accessed 4 April 2001].

5. Lawrence A. Cremin, ed. "Horace Mann's Legacy," in *The Republic and the School* (Teachers College Press, 1957), 8.

6. Cremin, *The Republic and the School*.

INDEX

ABOUT THE AUTHOR

Judy Breck attended Texas public schools, primarily in El Paso, completed a political science major at Northwestern University, and received her bachelor of arts from the University of Texas at El Paso. After one year of teaching high school, she alternated for several years between writing advertising copy in El Paso and staffing Texas political election campaigns in Austin. In 1968, a job on the national staff of Richard Nixon's presidential campaign brought her to New York City, where she has remained.

She was coordinator of the MENTOR program, which established educational partnerships between public schools and law firms. After having built the program in New York City, she facilitated its expansion nationwide. She also staffed six national Symposia on Partnerships in Education, sponsored by the White House to bring together people and projects striving to improve schools. In 1997, in an early effort to leverage the power of the Internet for learning, she led the creation of HomeworkCentral, a pioneering educational Web site that organized the educational content of the Web for students and researchers. She left that project in May 2001, shortly after her book *The Wireless Age: Its Meaning for Learning and Schools* was published by ScarecrowEducation. She spent the remainder of the year writing *How We Will Learn in the 21st Century* and building the book's complementary Web pages at www.EdClicks.com. She maintains a virtual studio at www.MediaWhatYouSay.com and is participating in the development of a wireless marketing enterprise.